Not as the Scribes

Not as the Scribes

JESUS AS A MODEL FOR PROPHETIC PREACHING

Ryan Ahlgrim

Foreword by Don M. Wardlaw

Herald
Press

Scottdale, Pennsylvania
Waterloo, Ontario

Library of Congress Cataloging-in-Publication Data

Ahlgrim, Ryan, 1957-
Not as the scribes : Jesus as a model for prophetic preaching / Ryan
Ahlgrim.
     p. cm.
Includes bibliographical references.
ISBN 0-8361-9200-1 (alk. paper)
1. Preaching. 2. Jesus Christ—Preaching. I. Title.
BV4211.3 .A42 2002
251—dc21

                                         2002000053

Unless otherwise noted, Scripture is from the *New Revised Standard
Version Bible*, copyright 1989 by the Division of Christian Education
of the National Council of the Churches of Christ in the USA, and is
used by permission, with all rights reserved.

To order or request information, please call
1-800-759-4447 (individuals); 1-800-245-7894 (trade).
Website: www.mph.org

To E. Joe and Emma Richards
who taught me the character of a preacher

Table of Contents

Foreword

Many preachers are on the move today. I refer not to clerical transit from parish to parish, country to city, or zeal to burnout. Rather, I speak of a mobility of the homiletical mind. Most preachers who care about preaching know that the pulpit world is living through a paradigmatic change in the understanding of preaching. For the past three decades the homiletical ground in the western world has been shifting from deductive toward inductive, from static toward tensive, from denotive toward connotive, from left brain toward right brain, from points toward moves, from objectivity toward evocation, from authoritarian toward relational, from isolation toward collaboration. Such continuums give us preachers coordinates for navigating our way through the sea changes in homiletical theory, schema for locating ourselves in the swirl of the pulpit revolution.

With this volume, *Not as The Scribes: Jesus as a Model for Prophetic Preaching,* Ryan Ahlgrim gives us yet another helpful spectrum for understanding possibilities in preaching that can trigger transformation of mind and spirit. Ahlgrim works on the continuum between what he terms *scribal preaching* and *prophetic preaching.* He finds in the preaching of the scribes in Jesus' day a type of religious discourse that, interestingly, mirrors a number of the traditional preaching models of our day. Scribal preaching couches its approach in appeals to the cognitive, concentrating a tight focus on isolated biblical texts, on the original setting and intent of those texts. Scribal preaching equates preaching with talking *about* texts more than *from* texts, with speaking from lofty, lone, and established positions of ecclesial authority.

Prophetic preaching, on the other hand, grounds its model in the preaching of Jesus. This preaching engages the whole person, heart, mind, and soul, in communication that is relational, dialogical, and communal. Prophetic preaching contributes to, and participates in, the chemistry of transformation. To offer the good news of the kingdom as Jesus did is to speak from the authority of personal and communal experience, to *enact* biblically-based themes. Prophetic preaching joins the chemistry of transformation because it arises from the dynamics of the transformed and transforming heart.

What gives special spark and moment to Ahlgrim's thesis is his personal identification with prophetic preaching. You'll find no smell of "the lamp" in his writing. He has discerned and developed his homiletical understanding amid the tosses and turns of life as a busy parish pastor. His speaking as one without authority *becomes* his authority, a surety interwoven with his personal experience, solid scholarship, common sense, and the presence of the Spirit.

A fun way to meet Ryan Ahlgrim in his homiletical house is to slip into this volume through the back door. You'll find him at home back there, in his five sermons that demonstrate prophetic preaching. In these sermons you *experience* prophetic preaching. You are energized by Ahlgrim's angle of vision. You hear his voice, delight in his creativity, chuckle with his humor. You feel his love for people, his passion for justice, his connection with Scripture. Here you see and feel prophetic preaching embodied, enfleshed in Ahlgrim's person and ministry. Once you have tasted of his sermons, then head for the front of the house. Turn from this *experience* of prophetic preaching to the apology for this preaching. After all, if such a sequence is the way revelation functions, it might not be a bad way to get acquainted with how Jesus' preaching worked.

    —*Don M. Wardlaw*
      Professor Emeritus of Preaching and Worship
      McCormick Theological Seminary

The explorer returned to his people,
who were eager to know about the
Amazon. But how could he ever put into
words the feelings that flooded his heart
when he saw exotic flowers
and heard the night-sounds of the forest;
when he sensed the danger of wild
beasts or paddled his canoe over
treacherous rapids?

He said, "Go and find out for yourselves."
To guide them
he drew a map of the river.
They pounced upon the map. They framed it
in their town hall. They made
copies of it for themselves. And all who had a
copy considered themselves experts on the
river, for did they not know its every turn
and bend, how broad it was
and how deep, where the rapids were
and where the falls?[1]

Two Ways of Knowing

This wonderful parable presents two ways of knowing: knowing *about* a subject, and *knowing* a subject. The first way of knowing comes through secondhand information while the other way of knowing comes through firsthand experience. These two ways of knowing are obviously different from each other, and yet we constantly blur them together and fool ourselves into thinking we truly know something when actually we have only been told about it.

How do we know God? We can either learn about God, or we can experience the reality of God's grace and activity in the world. For Christians, the Bible is the prime source of information about God. And yet, the actual purpose of the Bible is not to tell us about God, but to set us on a spiritual journey of awareness so that we come to know God for ourselves and make a covenant with the living God. Unfortunately, many Christians treat the Bible the way the map is treated in the parable: they become experts on the map but don't actually go on the journey. In fact, the map gets confused with the reality behind it so that the map actually hinders people from discovering the reality it describes.

When I was eight years old I thought I was an expert on dinosaurs because I had read a book about them. I figured I knew as much about dinosaurs as the person who had written the book, so that I was now qualified to write a book about dinosaurs myself. Why not? What other information did I need? I had all the basic facts. What else is there? It never occurred to me that those basic facts were only as good as the digging that lay behind them. The digging and touching of the bones is where the true knowing comes from.

Job is presented in the Bible as a blameless man who "feared God and turned away from evil." But when he was overwhelmed by meaningless suffering, he questioned everything he had been taught about God and criticized the orthodox lectures of his friends. Job demanded justice of God, though he despaired that he would ever get a fair hearing. But in his whirlwind of anguish, he finally experienced the presence and voice of God, and exclaimed: "I had heard of you by the hearing of the ear, but now my eye sees you" (Job 42:5). His previous knowledge of God, based on the best theology and information, was replaced with actual encounter, and only then did he become whole.

In my limited experience, sermons (mine included) have usually been examples of communicating knowledge about a subject rather than enabling listeners to actually know the subject. Typically, sermons talk about God instead of facilitating an experience of God. Sometimes this is because the preacher has not actually encountered God. At other times it is due to a lack of God-given nerve (what we might call inspiration). But also it is because of a confusion between the map (the Bible) and the reality it describes. Most preachers begin by picking out a piece of the map for analysis. They look for the most interesting locations and the most promising routes. They consult all kinds of scholarly resources about the map and make careful translations of its mysterious characters. And then on Sunday morning they present the congregation with the fruits of their labors, explaining the meaning of the map as clearly as possible, enhancing the message with humor and illustrations, so that everyone will understand at least one section of the map.

But such preaching, ultimately, misuses the Bible. We are not meant to become experts on the map, and the task of preaching is not to talk about the map and imagine its locations. The map has only one purpose: to guide us to a location so that we experience it for ourselves. This is also the task of preaching. So preaching should not so much tell us about the Bible as it should *be* a Bible—guiding listeners to the desired location so that they have their own experience of the reality behind the Bible. To put it another way: preaching, in its purest form, is not about the Word of God, it is the Word of God. The sermon is not a detailed study of a map bound in leather—it is the trip itself, even the destination.

This is how Jesus preached. In contrast to the scribes of his day who explained the correct understanding and application of Scripture, Jesus enabled his listeners to experience God's present reality and activity. He took them directly to the Amazon.

In this book I divide preaching into two contrasting forms: scribal and prophetic. The first talks about a subject, seeking to explain it and apply it; the second embodies the subject so that it is experienced by the listener. The former talks about God, the latter speaks for God.

The term "prophetic preaching" may be easily misunderstood since it is frequently used in two other senses. I am not referring to predicting future events through God's inspiration, nor am I referring to religiously motivated social criticism (although prophetic preaching may include either of these features). In this study, prophetic preaching is identified by two primary ingredients: it presumes to speak for God, being a human embodiment of God's Word for us now, and it facilitates an existential encounter with God or Scripture, rather than simply transmitting information.

It is this kind of daring and inspired preaching that ignited the church and continued fueling the first several generations of believers. The apostle Paul urged Christians in

Corinth to "strive for the spiritual gifts, and especially that you may prophesy" (1 Cor. 14:1). Paul was not referring to foretelling the future or criticizing injustices, but to preaching with the Holy Spirit's inspiration so that God would continue to speak directly to the church with God's own Word.

But as the church grew and the Christian faith developed traditions of its own, its preaching became less like Jesus' and more like the scribes'. Throughout the centuries, prophetic movements have sprung up to reinvigorate the church, but the dominant preaching style has remained scribal: scholarly analysis, explanation, and the rehearsing of biblical facts and traditions. When preaching becomes merely or primarily explanation and information, the church loses its immediate experience of God. Faith becomes a learned tradition rather than a spiritually transforming encounter with the living God.

This book grows out of a personal quest to find a way to preach which will facilitate genuine conversion and ongoing transformation. Along the way I have picked up a number of important lessons, but ultimately my quest has led me back to the example of Jesus. Despite the considerable distance in time and circumstances, Jesus remains the prime and most powerful model and inspiration for prophetic preaching.

And all of us, with unveiled faces, seeing the glory of the Lord as though reflected in a mirror, are being transformed into the same image from one degree of glory to another; for this comes from the Lord, the Spirit.

—2 Corinthians 3:18

CHAPTER ONE

A Personal Journey

When I was ten years old, I wrestled with two possible future vocations: becoming a preacher or becoming a spy. James Bond movies were all the rage and I became enthusiastic about the prospect of working for the CIA or some other covert organization. I read books about secret agents and ciphers, and I spied on everyone in the family. I imagined myself in communist Russia, carrying a miniature camera and concealed gun, stealing secrets for the benefit of my government.

On the other hand, I also yearned to be a preacher. I was awed by my pastor as he preached. He spoke about the most essential, mysterious, powerful, and wonderful thing in life: GOD. And he did not just speak about God, he seemed to speak for God. I do not remember any of his sermons, and I even lack a clear image of him preaching, but as a child I believed he had spoken with God and God had spoken with him, and what we were hearing from the pulpit was God's very message for us. I wanted such a relationship with God.

But there was a problem: becoming a spy and becoming a preacher appeared to be incompatible (unless I smuggled Bibles into Russia). One vocation harms one nation in order to help another, while the other vocation eschews such national selfishness. The spy is secretive and deceitful, while the preacher is open and honest. I could not have both, I needed to choose one or the other. Would it be excitement or ethical behavior, glamour or profundity? The noble, world-embracing vision of preaching decided the matter, and at the age of ten I promised God I would become a preacher.

My first taste of preaching came five years later when my church celebrated its annual Youth Sunday. The youth group selected me and my best friend to deliver a joint sermon (since we talked the most in Sunday school class). Following a week of preparation, we presented to the congregation fifteen minutes of, "How Do We Know There's a God?" It was a topical sermon rather than an exposition of Scripture, and it consisted of odd pieces of dubious evidence piled up for maximum effect. Afterward, the congregation warmly congratulated us on a fine job. My mother, never much of a churchgoer, came out of the sanctuary with tears streaming down her face and gave me a big hug. It was not a good sermon, but I thought it was, and it confirmed my desire to preach. It was exciting—as exciting as spying. From then on my pastors encouraged my theological and homiletical interests.

When I was in college I noticed a curious fact: I could easily listen to an hour-long lecture, hanging on every word, but I could not keep focused on a twenty-minute sermon. Five minutes into a sermon my mind would inevitably begin wandering. Now and then an illustration might bring me back, but only momentarily. It didn't seem to make any difference who the preacher was or how well he or she presented the sermon, I simply could not maintain the kind of attention I would give a college lecture.

I pondered this paradox for some time and finally came to the conclusion that the reason I could stay tuned to a lecture but not a sermon was because a college lecture generally contains new information whereas most sermons present old information. The content of a lecture, presented in a course I had never had before, could not be anticipated. On the other hand, I could guess the main points of most sermons simply by hearing the Scripture lesson and the first minute of exposition.

This realization could have led me to some awareness of the limitations of expository sermons in which the preacher primarily explains the meaning of a text and gives a few points on how it ought to be applied to our lives today. I could have begun to explore the possibility of prophetic preaching in which the preacher proclaims a bold new word grounded in the themes of Scripture and inspired by the presence of God's Spirit. Instead, I came to the conclusion that sermons ought to be good lectures: a lively presentation of new information and new ideas. In addition, I made a promise to myself that when I preached I would never bore a congregation the way I had felt bored countless times. Sermons are practically synonymous with boredom, but I was determined to make my sermons so provocative and interesting that even I could listen to them.

Following college, my church hired me as a youth pastor and I had the opportunity to preach from time to time. Whenever I preached, my oldest brother made a point of coming to church to listen even though he was an agnostic. I therefore made it my goal to preach sermons that would be meaningful and persuasive to him. This was a formidable challenge. It meant I had to cut out of my sermons stereo-typical language, easy answers, and unexamined beliefs. I once heard of a famous writer who told aspiring writers that if they wanted to be successful they needed a "built-in crap detector." My brother performed this function for me. Whenever I was writing a sermon, I imagined him looking over my shoulder critiquing every line. If it didn't pass his scrutiny, it didn't get preached.

In my first attempt at preaching after becoming youth pastor, I decided to give a topical sermon rather than an expository sermon. I figured a topical sermon would be less likely to be boring. The resulting sermon was thoroughly

theological as well as imaginative, but it made no reference
to the Bible. The Scripture lesson, which was read earlier in
the service, set the theme for the sermon but I did not exegete
the text or mention it in my sermon. After the service, one
young man came up to me and said, "That was the best sermon I ever heard!" I was elated. I thought I had found the
secret formula for the perfect sermon. My supervising pastor
was less enthused. The next day in her office she said to me,
"Next time preach a biblical sermon."

With this directive in mind, my next sermon was indeed
biblical. I took a passage of Scripture, examined it, interpreted it, and applied it to our lives. This sermon also
received its share of positive reviews. So from then on I
preached expository sermons on a regular basis. Although I
still indulged in the occasional topical sermon, I now regarded them with some theological suspicion. My thinking went
something like this: The Christian faith must be biblically
grounded, therefore sermons ought to have an explicit biblical core; otherwise, our faith may wander from its proper
anchorage, tempted by the exotic, fashionable, and faddish.
In addition, congregations appear to be increasingly biblically illiterate, therefore an expository sermon keeps knowledge
of the Bible more firmly in the mind and may even expand
that knowledge. And although an expository sermon may
run a greater risk of being boring, I was certain I could avoid
this problem by filling my sermons with jokes, stories, illustrations, and provocative cutting-edge biblical scholarship.

After serving my church as youth pastor for a year, I
entered seminary. During one of my seminary summers, I
worked as a counselor at a church camp. One evening a
guest pastor gave the chapel message to a group of ten-year-
olds. He began by reading the story of David and Goliath
from the King James Version of the Bible. As he read slowly
and awkwardly through the archaic language, I felt sinking
embarrassment for him. There was no way those ten-year-

old children could be following what he was saying.

But then, almost without a pause, he closed his Bible, laid it aside, and continued the story in his own words. He filled the sparse biblical narrative with colorful background and imagined conversations. He described the way a resentful David had to keep the flies off the peanut butter and jelly sandwiches as he brought them to the battle front for his older brothers. His voice took on different tones for the different characters and sneered when Goliath ridiculed David's challenge. He supplied sound effects as Goliath charged forward and David swung his sling round and round. He quickened the pace and built up the suspense. He described Goliath's fall and the surprised hush of the Philistines. And all of us listening to the story held our breaths to see if Goliath was only playing dead, waiting to grab David's leg when he drew too close.

I was astonished by the story. I found myself internally asking, "Are you allowed to do that—make up details and retell the story?" I had never before heard a dramatic retelling of a biblical story, and I was awed by the emotional impact it had on me, as well as the way it opened up new understandings of the biblical story.

Influenced by Stanley Hauerwas' thesis that foundational stories are the basis for the formation of our ethical character,[1] I concluded that the most effective preaching would be to retell biblical stories. Not only would the congregation find itself identifying with the story, and therefore have its character formed by the story, but it would also add to the congregation's cognitive understanding of the Bible. For many subsequent years, I preached a plethora of imaginative retellings of various biblical stories.

During my last two years of seminary, I worked as an assistant minister at a nearby church. The senior pastor was well known in the community for his gregarious and flamboyant personality. His preaching reflected his personality:

he never preached from behind the pulpit, but instead moved freely on the floor level, preaching without notes. His sermons were casual, down-to-earth, and salted with corny illustrations. And he always kept it very simple. As he told me more than once: "Tell them what you're going to tell them, tell them, and then tell them what you told them." I found his sermons easy to listen to, but not very deep or challenging. So I was puzzled that the congregation loved his sermons so much. Clearly he had the spiritual pulse of the congregation better than I did.

Sometimes he began a sermon with a brief, illustrative skit (and all special worship services contained dramas). He created them himself, in the barest outline, so that the participants needed to ad-lib most of their lines. All skits were done without rehearsal. Since I had some experience in writing church dramas, and I had always written them out in detail, I was surprised at how well his unpracticed improvised skits worked. The ad-lib effect gave them a fresh, natural quality.

All of these experiences prepared me as I left seminary and began my first pastorate, preaching every week. Unlike many of my peers, I relished the challenge of creating a new sermon that would energize my congregation every Sunday. Sermon preparation became my most important spiritual discipline as I regularly pondered Scripture passages, sought new questions to ask, and new ways to look at old verses. I had to examine my own life repeatedly, seek to be honest, bring structure out of chaotic truths, and find the best way to say it. I was never content with a mediocre sermon (though many were). I figured that since people were setting aside time to listen to me in the midst of their worship of God, I had an obligation to give them a message that truly mattered every week.

I gradually learned, through trial and error, better ways to begin a sermon, better ways to end a sermon, and better ways to communicate in the midst of the sermon. I learned what concerned my congregation and what did not. I learned what kind of theology was truly relevant to my church and what kinds were best left among the academics in seminary. And when it came time for my periodic pastoral evaluations, my congregation always gave me the highest marks in preaching.

Although I have always used a variety of approaches, over time I settled into a sermon pattern that worked well and came naturally to me, and so I used it (and still use it) frequently. I begin the sermon with a story, often from my own life. The story serves to introduce the main question or idea that the rest of the sermon will explore, and I state that question or idea at the conclusion of the story. This thematic statement is as terse as possible, and it is designed to either jar the congregation, pique their curiosity, or elicit an internal "yes, I know what you're talking about!" I then suggest that the Scripture lesson addresses this particular question or idea, and I launch into an exposition of the Scripture lesson, drawing out what I hope are a few creative insights which confirm, answer, or expand upon my thematic statement. Next I move to the present, suggesting how the biblical insights might be applied to some of our pressing situations. Finally, I conclude with a story that best illustrates the answers or themes I have developed.

This simple and flexible format communicates and applies biblical interpretations with ease and interest. It does not, however, guarantee a good sermon. The key to a good sermon lies more in its content and delivery than in its format. The stories need to be honest, engaging, and clearly illustrative. The theme of the sermon needs to be sharply articulated and of concern to the congregation; the exposition needs to be simple and creative. The application needs to be fair and genuinely helpful or challenging, and the delivery needs to be fluid, natural, and passionate. A preacher can use any format to be soul-searching and creative, or, more unfortunately, trite and ponderous. Thankfully, I was able to combine good content and delivery with my favored format over the years, and the congregation never fell asleep (except for one three-year-old boy who snored loudly).

But after ten years of preaching in this style, I became weary of explaining biblical texts and I felt something essential was missing. My first clue to what was missing came when I was invited to preach at an African-American church. I had visited the church the previous Sunday and watched the preacher shout and sing, clap his hands and jump up and down while his congregation cheered him on. I had never witnessed this type of preaching. The sermon had no recognizable structure but instead moved intuitively and extemporaneously, and rather than conveying information or ideas, or expositing Scripture, it was an almost pure expression of feelings.

The preacher was a friend of mine, and after the service he invited me to preach at his church the following Sunday. I accepted. That week I reviewed the sermons I had preached in the past three months and I picked out what I regarded as the best one. It was a sermon on the three temptations of Jesus when he was fasting in the wilderness. This has always been a favorite Scripture passage for me, and my sermon focused on the meaning of these three temptations for the church today. This sermon epitomized my goal of preaching a provocative and engaging expository sermon.

The following Sunday I stood before the congregation and delivered my well-rehearsed sermon. At first the congregation punctuated each statement I made with a "That's right" or a "Well" or an exclamation of praise. But as the sermon continued, the responses became fewer until halfway through the sermon they stopped all together. I was bombing, and I had no idea what I could do to reverse it, so I droned on to my conclusion. Following the service, each member of the congregation shook my hand at the sanctuary door. They were polite. Several made comments like, "That was interesting" or "I've never heard a sermon like that before." No one, however, congratulated me or expressed appreciation. One elderly woman stepped forward, took my hand and said, "I see you're a young preacher, so let me give you some advice. It isn't a sermon unless you preach the blood of Jesus."

This experience started opening my eyes to the limitations in my preaching. My early commitment to present new information and new ideas in my sermons (so as not to be boring) had resulted in sermons that were primarily teaching-oriented. Most of my sermons were inspiring Bible lectures. These could certainly be entertaining, helpful, and informative, but they spoke only to the cognitive mind—a tendency reinforced by using my agnostic brother as a sermon pre-viewer. His imagined skeptical scrutiny added thoughtfulness and integrity to my sermons, but it also made them primarily intellectual. I was not appealing to the feelings and intuitions of my congregation. In addition, I was narrowing my audience to one kind of listener—the intellectual doubter—and was not sufficiently addressing believers and those who were ready to become believers. Rather than honoring and celebrating faith, I was always trying to intellectually create it.

My pastor's advice to preach biblical sermons, although certainly good advice, also had potential pitfalls. It led me to preach sermons that centered on explaining biblical texts—a cognitive activity. I imagined that, if properly presented, everybody would be as interested in biblical history, archaeology, scholarship, and textual examination as I was. After all, dissecting a text and placing it in its historical or literary context can be great fun and deeply meaningful to the scholar. But the fact is, only a small minority of listeners are truly interested in textual archaeology, no matter how well presented. Most people are simply not historically or analytically inclined, and so sermons that depend on a cognitive analysis of a text are not going to speak to most people's spiritual needs. And even for those who do enjoy this kind of biblical study, it is still a cognitive rather than a spiritual experience.

Over the years, my congregation was certainly learning a lot about the Bible, and I am sure that my ideas and applications influenced some of their thinking and decision making. But for me the increasingly troublesome question was: Are they encountering God? Are they truly being spiritually transformed or am I changing only their thinking? Among the Sufis there is a saying that there are three ways to know fire: to hear about it, to see it, and to touch it. My congregation was hearing about fire every Sunday. I explained the fire to them with helpful information and genuine passion. But in my sermons they were not seeing the fire for themselves, and they certainly were not touching it.

My congregation was learning about the Bible but not necessarily living the Bible. Their minds were sometimes changed, but not their souls. I never sensed that through my sermons people were truly meeting the living Jesus Christ and experiencing a fundamental transformation of their being.

Perhaps I am wrong—perhaps people were encountering God but I could not see it since it cannot be quantified. But I never experienced the crowds being astounded, as the Gospel of Mark says they were when they heard Jesus. I know that no one was visibly responding with a changed life.

In seminary I was taught that 90 percent of sermons are didactic teaching, but that the best sermons ought to be a proclamation.[2] I embraced this idea, and fooled myself into thinking that my sermons were proclamations rather than Bible lectures. But when I saw examples of some African-American preaching, I began to realize how didactic I had always been. Proclaiming the faith is fundamentally different from explaining or describing or arguing the faith.

Proclaiming the faith conveys the experience itself. As someone has said, "No one ever got drunk hearing the word 'wine.' " A proclamation does not talk about wine but gives the wine to the congregation so the congregation can drink and become drunk.

As I became unsatisfied with my expository preaching (and exhausted with always explaining the biblical text), I often turned to more topical preaching, especially of a psychological or therapeutic nature. These sermons may have been helpful in their own way, but they were still information-laden discussions of a subject rather than a spiritual encounter. I still had not found what I was looking for.

I turned often to Mark's description of Jesus teaching with "authority, and not as the scribes" (Mark 1:22). How exactly did Jesus convey his message, and how was it different from the scribes? Could Jesus be used as a model for proclamatory preaching—a preaching that brings people into an encounter with God and opens up the potential for spiritual conversion? Could we, like Jesus, speak as prophets—bringing God's living voice into the here and now to speak to us?

And so I began seeking a new way of speaking. As Jesus once said, new wine cannot be put into old wineskins, or the skins burst. Instead, "one puts new wine into fresh wineskins" (Mark 2:22).

They went to Capernaum; and when the sabbath came, (Jesus) entered the synagogue and taught. They were astounded at his teaching, for he taught them as one having authority, and not as the scribes.

—Mark 1:21-22

CHAPTER TWO

The Scribes and Jesus

What was it exactly about Jesus' teaching that caused the crowds to be astounded? How did Jesus' authority differ from the authority exhibited by the scribes?

To answer these questions, we first need to have a basic understanding of the scribes. Unfortunately, we do not know much about the scribes in Jesus' society prior to the fall of Jerusalem in A.D. 70.[1] In the most literal sense, "scribe" means "writer." The word is used in the ancient world to refer to a broad range of people who write, take dictation, keep records, or act as government officials. Since scribes were literate, they were an educated elite, enjoying high social and political status. But aside from these broad generalizations, we are compelled to turn to the Gospels themselves to understand who the scribes are supposed to be.

In Mark, the scribes are usually associated with Jerusalem (3:21; 7:1) and represent the spiritual and political establishment of Judaism. They seem to function in two ways: first, as a sort of religious police force, investigating doctrinal correctness and orthodox practice (12:28ff.); and second, as authoritative religious teachers for the common people (9:11). The Gospel of Matthew portrays their basic role positively (23:1-3) as teachers of the predominant religious tradition. Luke introduces a new designation, "lawyer," which seems to be synonymous with "scribe" (10:25). The term lawyer clarifies another function of the scribes: they were experts in the law (which among Jews would mean the Mosaic Law). As such, they were official interpreters of Scripture. Most likely they engaged in the kind of elaborate exegesis which is developed later in the Talmud.

Since the ordering of Jewish society was closely based on Scripture (particularly Mosaic Law), it was necessary to have a group of people who could interpret the Scripture so it could be applied correctly to all the details of life. As new situations arose in society, the Scriptures needed to be consulted and interpreted to determine how to respond. The result was a slowly accumulating tradition of correct interpretations and applications that the Gospel of Mark refers to as "the tradition of the elders" (7:3, 5). In Jesus' day this tradition was still fluid and unwritten. Eventually, centuries after Jesus, this tradition became the massive and authoritative written Talmud of rabbinic Judaism.

The Gospel writers portray the scribes (along with the Pharisees) as being responsible for maintaining and passing on this growing oral tradition. Thus, the scribes were teachers whose authority derived from their position as government functionaries and their expert knowledge of an authoritative legal/religious tradition. We have no easy parallel to this in our society. A scribe would be a sort of combination Bible professor and government-sponsored lawyer.

So when Mark (and also Matt. 7:28-29) contrasts Jesus' authority and teaching style with that of the scribes, we at least have a general idea of what Mark was assuming about the scribes. The teaching of the scribes would have focused on a detailed exegesis of Scripture combined with an application based on an authoritative tradition. The style would have been logical and didactic, appealing to the hearers' cognitive functions and their respect for institutional authority.

Jesus' authority and teaching style were radically different.[2]

For the Gospel writers, one of the most obvious differences between Jesus' teachings and the scribes' teachings was the fact that Jesus rejected the authority of the oral tradition. Mark 7:1-23 provides us with the most stark picture of this contrast. When scribes asked Jesus, "Why do your disciples not live according to the tradition of the elders, but eat with defiled hands?" Jesus brushes off their complaint with a quotation from Isaiah and the statement, "You abandon the commandment of God and hold to human tradition" (Mark 7:5-8). Jesus goes on to criticize the tradition of Corban, a legal provision that allowed money to be dedicated to God which otherwise might be owed to others: "For Moses said, 'Honor your father and your mother'; and, 'Whoever speaks evil of father or mother must surely die.' But you say that if anyone tells father or mother, 'Whatever support you might have had from me is Corban' . . . then you no longer permit doing anything for father or mother, thus making void the word of God through your tradition. . . ." (Mark 10:9-13).

Jesus was not alone in criticizing particular legal opinions of elders from the past. The rabbis used some opinions in the tradition to argue against others, and in fact the tradition of Corban was eventually abandoned. But unlike the rabbis (and scribes), Jesus' authority to teach was not dependent on tradition. Scripture had authority, but the tradition did not.

This does not mean that Jesus always disagreed with the applications of the oral tradition. According to detailed studies by Bruce Chilton, Jesus found the traditions "positively valuable and useful."[3] Jesus' interpretations of some Scriptures were in agreement with the oral traditions. But unlike the scribes, Jesus did not quote the tradition to bolster his arguments; he did not use it as an authority. Instead, he felt free to disagree with it and disregard it whenever he chose to. The Scripture itself always took precedence over tradition.

Since Jesus gave authoritative priority to Scripture, one would expect Jesus to have engaged in detailed exegesis and explanation of Scripture as the scribes apparently did. But remarkably, Jesus' teaching did not primarily focus on interpreting Scripture either. This is the second most obvious difference between Jesus' teaching and that of the scribes. Scripture quotation is fairly rare in his teaching, and exposition of Scripture even rarer. Instead, Scripture functions as an all-pervasive spiritual background. Jesus argued from overarching biblical themes rather than details within verses. "Woe to you, scribes and Pharisees, hypocrites! For you tithe mint, dill, and cummin, and have neglected the weightier matters of the law: justice and mercy and faith. It is these you ought to have practiced without neglecting the others. You blind guides! You strain out a gnat but swallow a camel!" (Matt. 23:23-24).

On one occasion Jesus defended his disciples when they worked on the Sabbath, not by going into detailed exegesis of Deuteronomy 5:12-15, the Sabbath commandment, but by quoting the broad principle of mercy articulated in Hosea 6:6 (Matt. 12:1-7). In deciding how best to apply Scripture to particular situations, Jesus was guided less by logical analysis of phrases and words, and more by the biblical principle of loving God and loving one's neighbor (Mark 12:28-34). Interestingly, a scribe agreed with Jesus on this point, and Jesus found such agreement noteworthy enough to tell him, "You are not far from the kingdom of God."

Scripture provided Jesus with thematic touchstones and broad proofs for a message that was fully rooted in the present instead of the past. As Chilton writes, "He used Scripture as a starting point in his preaching, and therefore as a vehicle of his vision of God, but understanding Scripture was not for him the goal of preaching. His task, as he understood it, was not essentially interpretive."[4]

This brings us to the most crucial difference of all

between Jesus and the scribes: the teaching of the scribes was rooted in the past whereas Jesus' teaching was rooted in the present and the future. "The time is fulfilled, and the kingdom of God has come near" (Mark 1:15a). Jesus focused on what God is doing *now*. He was not concerned about giving lectures on Bible stories and explaining the meaning of past events. Instead, Jesus experienced God's story as continuing into the present. The long-awaited kingdom of God is drawing near, a new age dawning, with himself playing an active role in bringing it about: "But if it is by the finger of God that I cast out demons, then the kingdom of God has come to you" (Luke 11:20). Such a person does not focus his teaching on exposition of old stories but on sharing the new reality of which those stories spoke. This present and future orientation would have made Jesus' teaching truly astonishing compared to that of the scribes. "[N]either Jesus nor his followers was concerned to produce an extended exposition," claims Chilton. "Jesus seems to have broken new ground, not in contemporizing Scripture (which most intelligent preachers do), but in making God's present activity, not the text, his point of departure."[5]

Because Jesus experienced God acting decisively in the present, and because Jesus felt called to proclaim and enact this new reality, his teaching is filled with a personal authority. Unlike the scribes whose authority derived from expertly handling an authoritative tradition, Jesus believed his authority came directly from God (Mark 11:27-33). Thus, his words were, in some sense, God's Word. Jesus presumed so much authority derived from God that he felt authorized to reinterpret Scripture and announce God's intent for the new age: "You have heard that it was said to those of ancient times, 'You shall not murder'; and 'whoever murders shall be liable to judgment.' But I say to you that if you are angry with a brother or sister, you will be liable to judgment" (Matt. 5:21-22).

Some have regarded the six antitheses in Matthew 5 ("You have heard it said . . . but I say to you") as a normal form of rabbinic discourse on the law, but there are no true parallels in the Talmud for this construction, and the emphasis on personal authority is jarring and unmistakable.[6] On the other hand, some have claimed that the antitheses show Jesus replacing the Mosaic Law with a new and better law. But this is hardly tenable. Rather, Jesus most likely regarded all of the Mosaic Law as eternally valid (Matt. 5:17-18; Luke 16:17), but he claimed to know God's intention behind the written laws, and he felt authorized to intensify and perfect the law for the new age.[7]

Jesus gave Scripture the highest authority, and yet Jesus was not adverse to subordinating one passage of Scripture to another that more clearly revealed the original intent of God. On the subject of divorce, he did not strike down the Mosaic legislation in Deuteronomy 24:1, but claimed this was a concession to sin whereas Genesis 2:24 is the primary ethical guide (Mark 10:2-9).

Jesus would even press against a literal reading of the commandments in order to point out what God really desired. For instance, he allowed his disciples to break the Mosaic laws of not working on the Sabbath, but he did not view it as breaking the law since there was biblical precedence for humanitarian considerations (Mark 2:23-28). And Jesus subordinated the entire Mosaic code of what foods are or are not kosher to the greater concern of what internal attitudes defile us (Mark 7:14-23). Many scholars doubt that Jesus "declared all foods clean" as Mark claims since Peter was still committed to kosher laws in Acts 10. But it is at least characteristic of Jesus that moral considerations are more important than cultic ones. Jesus viewed his own words as having an extraordinary authority: "The queen of the South will rise at the judgment with the people of this generation and condemn them, because she came from the ends of the earth to listen to the wisdom of Solomon, and see, something greater than Solomon is here! The people of Nineveh will rise up at the judgment with this generation and condemn it, because they repented at the proclamation of Jonah, and see, something greater than Jonah is here!" (Luke 11:31-32).

What kind of a person dares to speak this way? What kind of authority is this? It is prophetic authority. Clearly Jesus considered himself to be—at least—a prophet, one who is filled with the present-speaking words of God. No wonder the crowds were astounded by his teaching and authority.

In Matthew 23:34 three kinds of teachers are enumerated: prophets, sages, and scribes. Scribes teach a tradition, repeating and reinterpreting the past. Sages teach wisdom, creating proverbs to guide moral life in the present. Prophets teach what God is doing and saying, speaking a new word from God. Based on these distinctions, Jesus' teaching was least like a scribe and most like a prophet.

But Jesus was not a prophet in the same mold as the Old Testament prophets. Unlike most of them, he never prefaced his statements with, "Thus says the Lord. . . ." He did not speak as if God were speaking in the first person singular through him. Instead, Jesus spoke for himself; it was simply assumed that God's inspiration was behind his words. Furthermore, although Jesus may have been inspired by visions (Luke 4:5-8; 10:17-18), his preaching did not consist of describing visions and dreams as we find in some of the Old Testament prophetic books. And finally, although Jesus called people to repentance and announced the judgment of God, unlike the Old Testament prophets his teaching also consisted of many proverbs and wisdom sayings. His style seems to have been more casual, dialogical, and less oracular than what we find in the Old Testament. In the previous quotation from Luke 11:31-32, Jesus compares himself not only to the prophet Jonah, but also to the wisdom of Solomon.

He apparently saw himself as a sort of prophet-sage combination.[8]

Despite these differences between himself and the Old Testament prophets, the crowds recognized his type of authority: "A great prophet has risen among us!" (Luke 7:16). He, along with John the Baptist, who spoke in a similar fashion, was commonly regarded as a prophet.

The prophet preaches in such a way that we are taken to God, and we meet God, and we hear God for ourselves. This is how Jesus preached, and the specific tools and methods he used is the subject of the next two chapters. He astonished his listeners with God's immediacy, an immediacy that made scribal teaching seem like secondhand religion.

But here is the ultimate irony: even though the Christian faith was founded on a person whose teaching was prophetic rather than an interpretation of tradition, his spokespersons today are usually satisfied with interpreting his tradition rather than speaking with the same prophetic authority Jesus did. In other words, the proclamation of the church has become almost entirely scribal—the very opposite of what Jesus announced and intended.

This certainly does not mean that we ought to abandon the scribal discipline. Before prophets can become true prophets they must undergo the labors of a scribe. Jesus' teaching reveals a long and intimate meditation on Scripture. Though he rarely exposits Scripture, he is deeply familiar with the intricacies of Genesis, the Mosaic law codes, the writings of the prophets, and the Psalms. The preacher's study of and familiarity with Scripture should be equally evident. But the task of preaching is not completed through scribal analysis or even creative application of Scripture. Preaching that reveals God's dawning reign and facilitates our spiritual transformation must also be prophetic: taking us to God to hear God's own Word for us.

When he was alone, those who were around him along with the twelve asked him about the parables. And he said to them, "To you has been given the secret of the kingdom of God, but for those outside, everything comes in parables; in order that

'they may indeed look, but not
perceive,
and may indeed listen, but not
understand;
so that they may not turn again and
be forgiven.'"
—Mark 4:10-12

CHAPTER 3

How Jesus Preached Prophetically: the Forms

To understand how Jesus taught, we need to examine his different kinds of teaching, or the various verbal forms he used. Setting aside some dialogue responses and a few odd statements, Jesus' teachings in the first three Gospels can be placed in three broad categories: discipleship instructions, eschatological pronouncements, and parables. These categories blend into each other and it is doubtful Jesus himself would have differentiated his teaching forms this way. But these categories can aid us in our pursuit of modeling our preaching after Jesus.

Discipleship Instructions

It is a commonplace for scholars to claim that Jesus typically spoke in metaphor. However, this overlooks the fact that the synoptic Gospels contain an enormous amount of teaching material that is not only devoid of metaphor but of any figurative illustration at all. The Jesus of the synoptic Gospels often spoke in direct language, and the bulk of those sayings fall within the broad category of discipleship instructions: "In everything do to others as you would have them do to you" (Matt. 7:12). "Do not judge, so that you may not

be judged" (Matt. 7:1). "For if you forgive others their trespasses, your heavenly Father will also forgive you; but if you
do not forgive others, neither will your Father forgive your
trespasses" (Matt. 6:14-15). "Give to everyone who begs
from you, and do not refuse anyone who wants to borrow
from you" (Matt. 5:42). "Love your enemies and pray for
those who persecute you. . . . For if you love those who love
you, what reward do you have? Do not even the tax collec-
tors do the same?" (Matt. 5:44, 46).

From this brief sampling, two characteristics of this direct
form of speech stand out: it tends to be in command form
and tends to be about ethical behavior. But not all of Jesus'
direct speech is in command form; it can also be a reasoning
discussion: "Suppose one of you has only one sheep and it
falls into a pit on the sabbath; will you not lay hold of it and
lift it out? How much more valuable is a human being than
a sheep! So it is lawful to do good on the sabbath" (Matt.
12:11-12). And not all of Jesus' direct language deals with
ethical behavior. For instance, Matthew 10:5-14 is a set of
missionary instructions without figurative language.

Even though Jesus frequently issues discipleship instructions in direct, discursive speech, not all of Jesus' instructions
are devoid of metaphor or illustration. Sometimes Jesus gives
a direct instruction accompanied by a memorable image or
illustration. For instance, Jesus' direct command not to
worry is followed by a variety of striking illustrations about
birds and wild flowers (Matt. 6:25-34). Similarly, Jesus illustrates how we can trust in God by using the moving image
of a father who gave his son bread and fish instead of a stone
and a snake (Matt. 7:9-11). He illustrates God's unmerited
grace by referring to the gift of sun and rain for the good and
the bad (Matt. 5:45). Jesus also gives examples of true and
false charity, prayer, and fasting (Matt. 6:1-18).

In addition to these vivid illustrations, Jesus also salts his
discipleship instructions with metaphors: "You are the salt of

the earth; but if salt has lost its taste, how can its saltiness be restored? It is no longer good for anything, but is thrown out and trampled under foot" (Matt. 5:13). "The eye is the lamp of the body. So, if your eye is healthy, your whole body will be full of light; but if your eye is unhealthy, your whole body will be full of darkness. If then the light in you is darkness, how great is the darkness!" (Matt. 6:22-23). "Follow me, and let the dead bury their own dead" (Matt. 8:22). "Those who are well have no need of a physician, but those who are sick" (Matt. 9:12). "Those who find their life will lose it, and those who lose their life for my sake will find it" (Matt. 10:39). "It is easier for a camel to go through the eye of a needle than for someone who is rich to enter the kingdom of God" (Matt. 19:24).

Sometimes it is unclear whether Jesus is using a metaphor or an illustration, but the difference is substantial for interpretation. "If anyone strikes you on the right cheek, turn the other also; and if anyone wants to sue you and take your coat, give your cloak as well; and if anyone forces you to go one mile, go also the second mile" (Matt. 5:39-41). If the images in this passage are meant as illustrations, then Jesus is telling his disciples to follow literally these examples. But if these images are metaphors, then Jesus is inviting listeners to explore the spiritual meaning of these symbols and to respond to conflict with a transformed attitude and consciousness rather than a literal turning of the cheek.

In addition to metaphor, Jesus also uses simile in his discipleship instructions: "See, I am sending you out like sheep into the midst of wolves; so be wise as serpents and innocent as doves" (Matt. 10:16). "Truly I tell you, unless you change and become like children, you will never enter the kingdom of heaven" (Matt. 18:3). "Everyone then who hears these words of mine and acts on them will be like a wise man who built his house on rock" (Matt. 7:24).

There is a significant difference between those discipleship instructions that use only direct language or illustrations, and those that use metaphors and similes. The latter group of teachings is less directive and more enigmatic, requiring hearers to make their own interpretations and applications. Sometimes Jesus' metaphorical instructions are so enigmatic they cannot be interpreted with confidence: "Do not give what is holy to dogs; and do not throw your pearls before swine, or they will trample them under foot and turn and maul you" (Matt. 7:6).

In summary, a large block of Jesus' teaching consists of a wide variety of instructions for how to do God's will, what I call "discipleship instructions." A substantial portion of this teaching uses unadorned, direct speech or direct speech accompanied by vivid illustration. But the other portion uses metaphors and similes, requiring more thoughtful interpretation. One characteristic all of Jesus' discipleship instructions have in common is that they are short, oftentimes only one sentence. Although the Gospel writers undoubtedly broke up some sayings and grouped together others, we do not find sustained discussions on single topics. It appears Jesus spoke briefly and abruptly. This has challenging consequences as we seek to use Jesus as a model for preaching.

Eschatological Pronouncements

One of the more contentious debates between scholars who specialize in the historical Jesus is whether Jesus was or was not eschatological.[1] For most of the twentieth century there was consensus that Jesus expected the future coming of the kingdom of God. In the last quarter of the century, scholars began doubting that Jesus was apocalyptic—expecting a sudden and violent end to history—since some of Jesus' parables seem to depict a gradual and hidden advent of God's kingdom. Toward the end of the century, some influential American scholars abandoned an eschatological Jesus altogether, believing instead that Jesus thought of God's kingdom as a continuous present possibility to be entered into now, rather than a future event.[2] But just as the noneschatological Jesus appeared to be dominant, voices rose once again in favor of an eschatological and apocalyptic Jesus.[3]

This discussion is not irrelevant to preaching. Should we conceive of God's kingdom as a present possibility or a future event, or some combination of both? Is it a political and social order, or an inner reality? How we answer these questions will have a tremendous impact on the content of our preaching and our overall theology. In my own opinion, there is overwhelming evidence that the historical Jesus expected God's kingdom to become a full and overwhelming reality sometime in the (near) future. There is also good evidence that Jesus saw the kingdom as present in a hidden way and that it could be entered into now by those with faith. Whether Jesus was apocalyptic—expecting a sudden and violent turning of the ages—I am less sure of, but it is a strong possibility.

Within the teaching of Jesus recorded in the first three Gospels there is a significant body of sayings that can be broadly categorized as eschatological pronouncements. Some of these sayings announce the presence of God's kingdom or the present fulfillment of God's promises (e.g., Luke 4:16-19; 11:20; 17:20-21), while others announce the nearness of God's kingdom and the future fulfillment of God's promises (e.g., Mark 1:15; 14:25; Matt. 5:3-10; 10:23; 16:28). In contrast to these positive pronouncements about the kingdom, there are negative pronouncements about future judgment and being left out of the kingdom (e.g., Matt. 5:21-23; 11:20-24; Luke 6:24-26).

All of these eschatological pronouncements are brief. Like Jesus' discipleship instructions, these are not extended discussions. Most use direct speech rather than metaphor, and yet ambiguity remains. Jesus is direct but not clear. What does it mean to say the kingdom of God is "at hand" or "has come near" (Mark 1:15)? Or what does it mean to say that some will see that the kingdom of God "has come with power" (Mark 9:1)? And what does it mean to say that the kingdom of God "is among you" (Luke 17:21)? Were these statements clear to the original hearers, or were they just as baffling and open to various interpretations as they are now?

Within the category of eschatological pronouncements is another body of sayings with a significantly different flavor and set of images. These are the apocalyptic sayings. Mark has collected most of these in one place, chapter 13, and Matthew and Luke also tend to lump them together (Matt. 24; Luke 21) although they can be found at the end of some parables as well (e.g., Matt. 13:40-43, 49). These apocalyptic sayings differ from the other eschatological pronouncements in that they announce a coming destruction, a cataclysmic turning of the ages, and perhaps an end to history. In addition, these sayings come as close to a continuous discussion on one topic as we find in the synoptic Gospels (at least, as presented in places such as Mark 13).

Whether we choose to include or exclude these apocalyptic sayings in our understanding of Jesus' preaching, it is still important for us to recognize that Jesus' preaching had an eschatological orientation. He fervently believed that God was at work in the present, bringing into reality heaven on earth and the wonderful rule of God. Jesus not only believed this, he experienced it and inaugurated it through his own ministry. This eschatological orientation, with its various pronouncements, shaped all the rest of his teaching. His discipleship instructions do not stand alone, but are completely undergirded by his confidence that God's will is triumphing in this world.

Parables

Jesus' third and most unique form of teaching was parables. His parables are closely associated with his similes and metaphorical sayings. What distinguishes a parable from these figurative sayings is that a parable narrates a plot. Rather than one image acting as a metaphor or simile, the entire story is the metaphor or simile: "With what can we compare the kingdom of God, or what parable will we use for it? It is like . . ." (Mark 4:30-31). Jesus' parables are also closely associated with his eschatological pronouncements since a good many of the parables are explicitly about the kingdom of God (e.g., Matt. 13:24, 31, 33, 44, 47). So Jesus' parables represent his most complex form of teaching, bringing together metaphorical instruction, eschatological pronouncement, and an extended narrative.

Jesus' parables share several common characteristics. In addition to containing a metaphor and a narrative, his parables are brief, realistic, surprising, and open-ended.[4] Scholars disagree as to whether Jesus' parables were brief when he first told them. On the one hand, the brevity of the parables as they are recorded in the Gospels seems to match the brevity of Jesus' other sayings. As they stand, they are marvelous examples of sharp, engaging stories. And since forgetting is the greatest tragedy in an oral culture, the shorter a parable, the more likely it will be remembered and faithfully passed on.[5]

On the other hand, the parables in the Gospels are so short and closely packed that they cannot be properly comprehended through one hearing. Some scholars suggest that the parables, as they appear in the Gospels, are in a compacted literary form that expects repeated readings, and that originally Jesus' parables must have been much longer, allowing listeners time to engage in the story.[6] John Dominic Crossan, who used to advocate for the original brevity of Jesus' parables, more recently admitted that they "may well be no more than plot summaries of stories which might have taken hours to tell."[7]

The debate over whether Jesus' parables were originally

brief or long is important if we are seeking to use Jesus as a model for preaching. At this point the question must be put on hold, but it is certainly true that in their canonical form, Jesus' parables are indeed all brief.

Realism is also basic to Jesus' parables. Although numbers and actions are sometimes exaggerated, the settings, characters, and plots are all taken from Jesus' own world or the commonly accepted after-world images of his culture. This realism is purposeful and essential, especially for parables referring to the kingdom of God. By using normal images for depicting the reign of God, Jesus seems to be emphasizing the reality and possibility of God's reign in our world.[8]

All of Jesus' parables contain a paradox or surprise. It may be a tiny seed becoming a big bush, a Samaritan helping a Jew, a rich and secure man losing everything, a one-hour worker receiving a full day's pay, or a dishonest manager being commended. But the surprises are not all of the same type or quality. They range from ecstatic joy to disturbing offense. It is as if Jesus were warning his hearers that the kingdom is completely unexpected, and that along with the joy there will be considerable shock.

Finally, Jesus' parables are open-ended. Hearers are implicitly invited to complete the parable, sometimes because the story has no ending (e.g., will the older son come inside and embrace the prodigal son?), but also because the metaphorical character of a parable requires the hearers to interpret it for themselves. Two parables are given extensive interpretations in the Gospels: the parable of the soils (e.g., Matt. 13:18-23) and the parable of the weeds in the wheat (Matt. 13:36-43), but it is highly unlikely that these interpretations are original to Jesus. Close examination reveals that the interpretations are not entirely consistent with the parables and they turn the parables into allegories. In any case, the interpretations are given only to an inner circle of disciples; general hearers are given no interpretations and must interpret for themselves (Mark 4:11, 34). A parable told by Jesus is meant to leave "the mind in sufficient doubt about its precise application to tease it into active thought."[9]

This brings us to the question: Why did Jesus use parables? How do they function in his overall teaching and preaching? The first common misconception that must be corrected is that Jesus' parables are allegories. Parables and allegories function in two entirely different ways. An allegory is a story in which each character or object represents something else. Once you know what each element symbolizes, the meaning of the story is clear and straightforward. For instance, C. S. Lewis' *Chronicles of Narnia* tend to be allegories (particularly the first book, *The Lion, the Witch, and the Wardrobe*). The lion, Aslan, is Christ; the White Witch is Satan or the forces of evil; Aslan's death and resurrection are Christ's death and resurrection, etc.

A parable, on the other hand, is not a collection of individual symbols put into a narrative. Instead, a parable functions as one symbol or metaphor. The story is the symbol rather than the individual characters or objects in the story. For instance, in the parable of the good Samaritan, the robbers are not meant to be symbolic of something else (e.g., demons, illness, misfortune), nor do the priest and Levite represent anything but themselves. The Samaritan is not a symbol of anything other than what he actually is—a despised heretic, and the innkeeper is not symbolic of the church or God. The individuals in this parable are not codes for something else, and the meaning of the parable is not in the parts. Rather, the meaning of the parable is conveyed by the story as a whole. Only when one has heard the whole story may the listener say, "Aha!"

Another example is the parable of the soils. All three synoptic Gospels give it an allegorical interpretation: the sower is presumably God, the seed is the Word of God, the four soils are four kinds of hearers of the word (or four different conditions for hearing the word), the birds are Satan, the rocks are persecution, and the thorns are the distractions of the world. Interpreted this way, the story is a cautionary tale for believers, warning them against falling away from the faith. But what would happen if we interpreted this story as a parable, ignoring all the supposed symbols and listening to the story as a whole? If the whole story is a metaphor for the kingdom of God, then it seems to be saying that the kingdom of God many times fails to emerge in our world, but do not lose hope because it will eventually emerge and make up for all failures.

This illustrates another difference between allegories and parables: allegories are easily understood once the symbols are decoded, but a parable cannot be simply decoded. Since the entire story is a metaphor, its meaning is always less clear and open to various interpretations. Because of this characteristic, parables cannot be reduced to a simple descriptive meaning (despite my attempt to do so above with the parable of the soils). An allegory can be explained, in fact is meant to be explained, not so with parables. As Bernard Scott says, "To undertake an exposition of parables runs counter to the very nature of parable. Exposition seeks to explain, to contain, and in that effort risks substituting what is not parable for parable. Not only can a parable's richness not be exhausted but its form is such that it subverts the effort at control."[10]

The position that Jesus' parables never act as allegories may be an overstatement. I do not doubt that in some of Jesus' parables certain characters may represent God, and some of Jesus' shorter parables have simple, symbolic elements (Matt. 13:44-45). But overall it is important to see Jesus' parables functioning as a complex yet unified metaphor.

Another common misconception is to think of Jesus'

parables as illustrations. In Western modes of communication we generally represent our theological thoughts in the form of abstract statements which we then clarify with an illustration. The illustration exists only as a way of assisting abstract communication. But a parable is not an illustration to assist some other, more direct, form of communication. A parable stands by itself. It is the communication.[11] The parable creates in the listener an experience that cannot be conveyed in an abstract statement. Jesus' parables mediate a religious experience of the kingdom of God. They do not so much talk about the kingdom as give listeners an opportunity to imaginatively enter the kingdom and taste it for themselves.[12]

From this it follows that parables do not primarily convey ideas. As Donahue says, "The parables are not carriers of ideas where the image is the husk to be discarded in the quest for the kernel of meaning."[13] This is not to say that ideas cannot be pulled out of a parable—they can and have been by centuries of interpreters. But the ideas cannot replace the parable, because the parable creates an experience of truth or reality that cannot be replicated by voicing mere ideas.

Ideas and images (stories) affect us in different ways. Ideas affect us cognitively—they speak to our thinking mind and our conscious ego. But images affect our feelings and intuitions—they speak to our unconscious. According to Jungian thought, images are the language of the unconscious, and images connect us to each other. And so the use of images taps into the unconscious, enabling effects on the human being that are more profound than ideas can accomplish. As Elizabeth Achtemeier says, "If we want to change someone's life from non-Christian to Christian, from dying to living, from despairing to hoping, from anxious to certain, from corrupted to whole, we must change the images, the imaginations of the heart."[14]

A final misconception is that Jesus' parables are moral example stories. Because parables are realistic, they can be read literally as well as metaphorically. When read literally, we have a tendency to look for "the moral of the story." Now the characters become examples of morality or immorality. But some of Jesus' parables, particularly the parable of the dishonest steward (Luke 16:1-8), become utterly nonsensical when read this way. Luke in particular seems to look for "the moral of the story" and attaches meanings to parables that seem unnatural (e.g., Luke 10:36-37; 16:9).[15]

Recently one scholar has proposed reading Jesus' parables as immoral example stories, which point out the injustices of peasant life.[16] According to this view, Jesus used his parables to unmask the social and economic oppression faced by the peasantry. The rulers and masters in Jesus' parables, so often seen as symbols of God, are actually realistic descriptions of despotism and oppression. This interpretive approach may help us be more sensitive to how these stories were experienced by peasants, but I think it is a mistake to read the parables literally instead of as metaphors.

So if Jesus' parables are not allegories, illustrations, ideas, or moral/immoral examples, what are they? They are metaphors; and at least the majority of them are metaphors for God's kingdom which is mysteriously and surprisingly entering into this world, compelling us to make life and death choices and run the risk of faith. Through these parables, Jesus was enabling people to see a reality more real than the status quo; he was helping them experience and enter into God's kingdom; he was empowering them to live out God's kingdom now through radical faith and self-giving love.

This explanation of the purpose and function of parables appears to differ from the one given in Mark: "To you has been given the secret of the kingdom of God, but for those outside, everything comes in parables; in order that 'they may indeed look, but not perceive, and may indeed listen, but not understand; so they may not turn again and be forgiven" (4:10-12). A literal reading of this quote might lead us to conclude that Jesus spoke in parables so that the crowds would not comprehend and enter God's kingdom. But such a reading is nonsensical. Why then speak to the crowds at all? Why bother with parables? Clearly this was not Jesus' (or even Mark's) understanding.

The lines quoted by Jesus are from Isaiah 6:9-10 and follow immediately on Isaiah's call to be a prophet. In its original context, the statement is meant to be fatalistic about the possibility of Isaiah's hearers responding with repentance, not that he is speaking in order to block understanding and repentance. Jesus uses this statement from Isaiah to give us a perspective on how parables function: they are not clear, direct communication, but they require the hearer to participate in the parables. Only if the hearer responds with faith—believes in and enters the kingdom—will the parable have done its revealing work. Thus, parables both conceal and reveal; the key (or secret) is faith. Matthew and Luke almost certainly understand the parables in this way and it is reflected in the way they soften the Isaiah quotation (Matt. 13:10-15, Luke 8:9-10). And it seems probable to me that Jesus understood his parables in this way as well. Incidentally, the fact that the Gospel writers use a quotation from Isaiah's calling to explain Jesus' parables suggests that they (and Jesus?) regard parables as a prophetic way of speaking.

With many such parables (Jesus) spoke the word to them, as they were able to hear it; he did not speak to them except in parables, but he explained everything in private to his disciples.

—Mark 4:33-34

CHAPTER 4

How Jesus Preached Prophetically: the Modes

This statement contains several puzzles. Did Jesus have two different modes of teaching—a public one and a private one—in which the first was enigmatic and the second was explanatory? When Jesus taught in public, did he always speak in parables? And what does Mark mean by "parables"?

Now that we have surveyed the forms of Jesus' oral teaching and preaching, we need to consider the modes in which he communicated with people. Along the way we may find the answers to the puzzles Mark offers us.

First of all, and perhaps most frequently, he communicated dialogically, one-on-one or with a handful of people. The Gospels often portray Jesus teaching while dining in someone's home (e.g., Luke 5:29-31, 7:36-50, 10:38-42, 11:37-52, 14:1-24, 15:1-2, 19:5-10). On these occasions the teaching appears to have been a give-and-take with a mixture of questions, answers, and short discussions. The Gospels also show Jesus being approached by individuals who engage Jesus in conversation, resulting in teaching (e.g., Luke 9:57-62, 10:25-28, 11:27-28, 12:13-15, 17:20-21, 18:18-25).

These intimate conversations with individuals and small groups are a natural setting for Jesus' brief proverbs, instructions, and pronouncements. The teaching would not have been a sustained sermon, but sporadic and dialogical.

Perhaps more sustained would have been his frequent teaching in synagogues (e.g., Luke 4:31, 44; 6:6; 13:10). This setting would have been more formal than dinner table discussion and presumably would have involved a larger number of people. One might suppose that in the synagogues Jesus preached what we would call sermons. But if our image is of an uninterrupted twenty-minute presentation from a raised platform, we are almost certainly wrong. Even in the synagogue, teaching was done from a sitting position (Luke 4:20) which invited informality and dialogue. We should assume that Jesus' teaching in the synagogues was also conversational and participatory. However, Jesus must have gone to the synagogues with a teaching purpose in mind, and therefore he must have been prepared to give instruction, tell stories, and make pronouncements. It would not have been simply extemporaneous, as it might have been at a dinner table or in a one-on-one conversation. Jesus had a message he wanted to give, and it must have had some sort of pre-planned shape and format.

Another setting for Jesus' teaching was to large crowds. One can argue that the setting for, say, the Sermon on the Mount (Matt. 5-7) is artificial, but the evidence that Jesus addressed large outdoor crowds is strong (e.g., Mark 4:1, 8:1-2, Luke 14:25). How did Jesus teach in these settings? Again, Jesus' teaching was probably more dialogical than we would imagine. Congregations sitting quietly in a sanctuary while the preacher preaches was not part of ancient Jewish culture. Many of the one-on-one conversations were probably interruptions while Jesus addressed crowds (e.g., Luke 11:27; 12:13). Even so, Jesus must have had something planned to say to the crowds, and what he said must have taken a lengthy period of time or a crowd would have never gathered to hear him. This is particularly clear in the episode of Jesus getting into a boat to teach crowds on the lakeshore (Mark 4:1). Teaching from a boat to a crowd on the shore does three things: it separates the speaker from the audience making dialogue nearly impossible, it uses water to amplify the speaker's voice so as to be heard by a very large crowd, and it requires a long presentation to make the whole effort worthwhile.

So we must conclude that at least on some occasions Jesus addressed large crowds in a sustained, nondialogical way. But if his teaching, as recorded in the synoptic Gospels, consisted entirely of short instructions, pronouncements, and very brief parables, how did he speak in a lengthy, uninterrupted way?

Matthew answers this question by giving us the Sermon on the Mount. But this discourse is obviously an artificial construction. English translations which cannot distinguish between second person singular and second person plural ("you") obscure the fact that the sayings in the Sermon on the Mount are addressed to different audiences—sometimes one person (5:29), sometimes many (5:28). Furthermore, the Sermon on the Mount doesn't really work as a sermon; it jumps from subject to subject too quickly. Many preachers have memorized or paraphrased the Sermon on the Mount and presented it to their congregations, and they can all testify that it's not a good sermon.

So how did Jesus shape his preaching when addressing a large crowd for perhaps several hours? Mark says it was with parables (4:1-34), and he almost certainly must be right, except the parables must have been much longer than the ones preserved in the Gospels. It is simply inconceivable that Jesus could have sustained a presentation to a crowd with a long string of very short parables. Nor could he have interspersed short instructions and proclamations among short parables; the result would have been too choppy and fast for an audience to hear and digest. If Jesus was indeed a popular teacher who drew crowds, then he must have had an effective way of speaking in a sustained manner. The only real possibility, based on information from the Synoptics, is that Jesus told long parables as the backbone of his sermons.

As we have already seen, all of the parables in the Gospels are short. However, it is quite possible that at least some of these parables were originally much longer, and that only the barest outlines were passed on for a couple of generations until finally being written down by the Gospel writers. It is easy to imagine the parable of the prodigal son (Luke 15:11-32) as a much longer story. The plot has enough complexity to sustain an entire sermon—as many preachers who have creatively retold it can testify. The parable of the dishonest steward (Luke 16:1-8) may also have been much longer, as well as the parables of the great dinner (Luke 14:16-24), the pounds (Luke 19:12-27), and the rich man and Lazarus (Luke 16:19-31). On the other hand, some of Jesus' parables have only the barest plot and work best by being very short, such as the mustard seed (Matt. 13:31-32), the hidden treasure (Matt. 13:44), and the pearl (Matt. 13:45). These parables would work better in dialogical situations such as the dinner table, although they could have been added sparingly to a longer presentation.

But Jesus' presentations would probably not have consisted entirely of parables. Preachers know from experience that communication, and overall effect, are improved by interspersing stories and statements. Jesus' longer "sermons," such as might have been preached from a boat near the shores of the Sea of Galilee, could possibly have consisted of an eschatological proclamation (such as the Beatitudes at the beginning of the Sermon on the Mount), followed by one or two long parables of the kingdom of God, each of which might have been complimented by some discipleship instructions, and concluding perhaps with a word of warning or a cautionary tale (such as concludes the Sermon on the Mount). This is of course speculation. No one knows the shape of Jesus' sermons (if he did indeed preach sermons). But the evidence at hand, combined with practical considerations, leads to a conclusion similar to the outline above.

My suggestion that Jesus preached to the crowds with long parables along with shorter proclamations and instructions raises a problem introduced at the beginning of this chapter. Mark claims that Jesus spoke to the crowds only in parables (4:34). But the Greek word for parable, *parabole*, refers to all kinds of figurative speech. This is true as well for the Hebrew word *mashal*, which is also translated as parable in the Old Testament. *Mashal* and *parabole* cover the entire range of metaphorical speech, from riddles and proverbs to stories. As we have seen, much (but not all) of Jesus' discipleship instructions make use of metaphors, similes, and illustrations. All of these would have been considered "parables" by Mark, and indeed some of the sayings in Mark 4, addressed to the crowd, are metaphorical instructions, not parables with plots (4:21-22, 23, 24-25).

But Mark poses one more problem. He says that Jesus spoke to the crowds in parables (figurative speech requiring interpretation by the hearers), but to his disciples "he explained everything in private" (4:34). Is it possible Jesus had two different kinds of teaching for two kinds of audiences: parables and figurative teachings for the crowds, and straightforward instructions or explanations for his inner circle of disciples? Many scholars balk at this suggestion since parables are not to be explained but experienced. While that is true, it does not rule out the possibility that for those who had already taken the step of faith to follow him and enter the kingdom, Jesus was willing to give further explanations about his parables as well as what it meant to live in the kingdom of God. In fact, this is most probable since these were the people who were around him night and day, most likely asking whatever questions came to their minds. It is difficult to imagine Jesus *not* giving further explanations to a close group of followers.

The Gospels are explicit that certain kinds of teaching were meant only for the disciples, such as the missionary instructions (Matt. 10:5-42). Even the Sermon on the Mount is addressed to his disciples rather than the crowds (Matt. 5:1-2). This makes sense since the Sermon on the Mount is filled with the most direct, straightforward discipleship instructions. It is completely natural to suppose that Jesus would have spoken primarily in pictures to the large crowds, but much more directly, and with more explanation, in his one-on-one conversations with his disciples. This is parallel to what happens today in many churches: the preacher speaks in broad terms and stories during the sermon, but then addresses specific questions and issues in the adult Sunday school class of committed learners.

"They were all amazed, and they kept on asking one another, 'What is this? A new teaching—with authority! He commands even the unclean spirits, and they obey him' " (Mark 1:27).

One more element of Jesus' prophetic preaching often overlooked are his healings and other symbolic acts. Mark cleverly weaves together an exorcism story and a teaching story in 1:21-27, and by doing so he suggests that at the heart of Jesus' teaching was his power to enact transformation. Words are cheap. Mark repeatedly refers to Jesus teaching the people, but records far fewer teachings than any other Gospel. Why? Perhaps because, for Mark, Jesus' *actions* were his teaching.

We tend to think of Jesus' healing or exorcism ministry as parallel to, but different from, his teaching ministry. Mark makes no such distinction. In another wonderfully blended story, Jesus forgives (but does not initially heal) a paralyzed man (Mark 2:1-12). The scribes are shocked by Jesus' arrogance—who can forgive sins but God alone? Jesus asks them which is easier, to forgive the man or heal him? And then to prove he does have the authority to forgive sins, he heals the paralytic.

Interpreters are often confused by this story. Jesus' question as to which is easier—to forgive or to heal—seems nonsensical. Forgiving and healing are separate activities, and if one is harder than the other, it's probably forgiving. The scribes' feeling of offense is justified—we may forgive those who sin against us, but what authority do we have to forgive sins committed against another? Overall forgiveness truly is the prerogative of God alone. For Jesus to forgive the paralytic is indeed "harder" than healing him. So healing him proves nothing regarding the authority to forgive.

But the key to understanding this story lies in the fact that Jesus' culture generally believed that illness was due to sin (e.g., John 9:1-2) *and that healing could not occur until the sin was forgiven.* The Babylonian Talmud declares, "No sick person is cured of his disease until all his sins are forgiven him." So when Jesus healed the paralytic, this was proof that the man's sins were already forgiven. It *is* harder to heal than to forgive, because the healing must be based on forgiveness.

This story throws a dramatic light on the meaning of Jesus' entire healing ministry. He was not simply curing people's physical ills, he was doing something spiritually more profound—he was symbolically freeing them from all of their sins. When he healed people he was in effect telling them that all their bonds were broken and they were free to enter God's kingdom. Mark is right: Jesus' healing actions *do* constitute his teaching.

Jesus' exorcisms perform a similar symbolic teaching function. Jesus explicitly says, "If it is by the finger of God that I cast out demons, then the kingdom of God has come to you" (Luke 11:20). Each time he freed someone from the inner control of evil and insanity, he was showing that Satan's kingdom on earth is being invaded by God's kingdom. God is establishing a beachhead in our world and God will soon reign over all. Or, to use Jesus' own analogy, the strong man is tied up and his house is being plundered (Mark 3:27).

So it is a mistake to think of Jesus' healings and exorcisms separately from his prophetic preaching. His deeds were prophetic deeds with prophetic meaning and teaching. Like Elijah and Elisha before him, he performed wonders that symbolized the presence and power of God. It was following a remarkable healing that the crowd concluded, "A great prophet has risen among us!" (Luke 7:11-16).

But Jesus' symbolic prophetic activity was not limited to healing and exorcism. Riding into Jerusalem on a donkey was a symbolic act reinforcing his message; overturning tables in the temple courtyard was a symbolic—not practical—act; and at his last supper he performed another symbolic act which became the church's ritual of communion. Just as Jeremiah wore a yoke to symbolize his message that the people of Jerusalem would be captured, and just as Isaiah went about naked to symbolize the imminent capture of Egypt and Ethiopia, so Jesus used symbolic acts to make real his prophetic preaching.

The desire to be like Jesus and not like the scribes . . . can lead to consequences which violate the intent of the Marcan text and God's will for interpreters. . . . (Jesus Christ) is the one who can speak with direct authority. We interpreters remain essentially in the position of the scribes, dependent on a prior authority and responsible to a scriptural tradition. We deceive ourselves and those we teach if we try to deny these limitations.

—Lamar Williamson Jr.[1]

CHAPTER 5

Ought We to Speak as Jesus Spoke?

Before proceeding to the task of using Jesus as a model for prophetic preaching, we need to examine carefully several serious objections and possible limitations. First is the obvious objection that we are not Jesus Christ, the Son of God in whom "all the fullness of God was pleased to dwell" (Col. 1:19). This is true, and any preacher who thinks otherwise is outside the biblical Christian faith. But this objection assumes that Jesus Christ spoke by his own authority and only he is allowed to do so. This assumption is false. Jesus did not speak by his own authority. The Gospels consistently portray Jesus as one who constantly submitted to the will and authority of God. Even the Gospel of John, which has the highest Christology of any of the Gospels, is careful to point out that Jesus does nothing on his own authority: "Very truly, I tell you, the Son can do nothing on his own, but only what he sees the Father doing" (John 5:19).

When Jesus healed someone, it was never by his own power but by God's power. When Jesus spoke, it was never by his authority, but by God's. Jesus experienced God guiding, inspiring, and empowering him. And even with his extraordinary experience of God's presence and power, Jesus never assumed he was free to ignore or overturn Scripture.

He felt guided to interpret Scripture and reveal God's deepest intent, but he never denied Scripture's authority (Matt. 5:17-19). Like all Christian preachers today, Jesus also had to submit to the authority of Scripture.

Did Jesus speak with an astonishing direct form of authority? Yes. But Jesus did not claim this authority exclusively for himself. He explicitly passed it on to those who had committed themselves to the kingdom of God: "Then Jesus called the twelve together and gave them power and authority over all the demons and to cure diseases, and he sent them out to proclaim the kingdom of God and to heal" (Luke 9:1-2). Luke also records Jesus sending out seventy missionaries, and they returned exclaiming, "Lord, in your name even the demons submit to us!" (10:17). Jesus spoke in God's name, and we are empowered to speak in Jesus' name. This does not mean we may only quote Jesus, anymore than Jesus was limited to quoting the Old Testament. To speak in Jesus' name means that we are not speaking out of our own goals or self-centeredness, but for God's purposes as we have met God through Jesus Christ. It is no longer we who live, but it is Christ who lives in us (Gal. 2:20), and when we speak it is with the sincerest intention that we are speaking with the Spirit of Christ in us (1 Cor. 7:25, 39-40).

Jesus is the ultimate embodiment of the character and presence of God, but speaking with authority is not unique to Jesus. He shares this way of speaking with all prophets. This is what makes a prophet identifiable as a prophet (whether a true or a false one): speaking directly a message from God. Within the New Testament we can find numerous examples of others who spoke with authority in a manner quite similar to Jesus himself. Three letters in particular are good examples of prophetic-style sermons: Philippians, James, and 1 John. We must keep in mind that when these letters were written, they were not Scripture. They were simply intended as sermons for Christians in early congrega-

tions. Thus, it is surprising to find these authors making pronouncements to their congregations in which reference to or
exposition of Scripture is almost entirely absent. Instead,
grounded in the themes of Scripture and the ministry of
Jesus, these authors speak for God in a fresh way, focusing
almost entirely on the present and future. Indeed, these letters most likely became Scripture because they functioned
prophetically, facilitating the congregation's direct encounter
with God.

One might object that the letters in the New Testament
possess a unique authority that the modern preacher cannot
assume, and besides, preachers (by and large) are not
prophets. After all, how many have had a calling such as
Isaiah's (Isa. 6:1-8) or Ezekiel's (Ezek. 1-2)? But to restrict
the prophetic guild to biblical authors or to those with extraordinary visions is far too limiting. Paul assumes that every
house church in Corinth has at least two or three prophets
among them (1 Cor. 14:26, 29).

But what does Paul mean by "prophets" and "prophecy"? Is he referring to the same type of speech that made
Jesus so astonishing? For Paul, speaking prophetically means
speaking "to other people for their upbuilding and encouragement and consolation" (1 Cor. 14:3). Speaking prophetically also has a confrontational role: prophets see into the
inner being of those standing outside God's kingdom and
challenge them in such a way as to elicit the possibility of
conversion and transformation (1 Cor. 14:24-25). Prophetic
speaking is a form of speech that is rational and understandable, as well as inspired by God (1 Cor. 14:18-19, 26).
Prophets in Paul's churches do not begin by saying, "Thus
says the Lord" (not even Jesus spoke this way), nor are they
so overcome by inspiration that they cannot control what
they say (1 Cor. 14:32-33). Nevertheless, it is a special form
of speaking, distinguishable from speaking wisdom or
knowledge (1 Cor. 12:7-10); and a prophet is distinct from

(and has more authority than) a teacher (1 Cor. 12:28-30). Although Paul's understanding of prophetic speech has its own unique nuances, it still conforms to our basic definition of prophetic speech:

* it speaks for God rather than explaining a tradition about God

* it facilitates an encounter with God rather than merely transferring information (which is what Paul would call "teaching").

For Paul, prophets are not unique individuals marked from birth; they are simply believers who have been given a gift by the Spirit. Like all gifts, the gift of prophecy can be prayed for, encouraged, practiced, and developed. It is a gift Paul wishes everyone would pursue (1 Cor. 14:1), and it is possible for all believers to exercise this gift (1 Cor. 14:24, 31).

Speaking prophetically, though, is problematic for the church. How do we know if the person is really speaking for God or not? How do we know if this is a message inspired and guided by God's Spirit, or just an ego-trip? And what are we to suppose when two "prophetic" preachers preach diametrically opposed messages on an important social issue?

Prophetic preaching is not inerrant preaching; it is human speech hoping and striving to be sensitive to what God is saying and doing now. Even though it speaks "with authority," its authority is actually no greater than what is discerned by the hearers. It is the hearers who are, or are not, astonished. It is the hearers who experience, or do not experience, truth being spoken. The apostle Paul instructs more than one congregation to weigh and test what the prophets say (1 Cor. 14:29; 1 Thess. 5:20-21). He acknowledges that speaking prophetically is bound to be imperfect in this world (1 Cor. 13:9-10).

In this regard, scribal preaching faces the same dilemma as prophetic preaching. Not only is our prophecy imperfect, as Paul says, but so is our knowledge. Some Christians would regard scribal preaching as "safer," more restrained, more accurate, more reliable, and therefore superior to prophetic preaching. But intensive exegesis and explanation of Scripture is no guarantee of truthfulness in a sermon. Scripture scholars legitimately debate the "intended meaning of the author" in practically every verse, and matters get enormously convoluted when scholars attempt to relate contradictory passages or seek to interpret the Scripture for our present situation. History shows all too clearly that the most sincere and orthodox exegetes still arrive at diametrically opposed interpretations and applications. In short, there is no consensus among honest interpreters about the meaning of Scripture. Like prophetic preaching, scribal preaching is subject to the limitations of culture, current knowledge, and spiritual maturity.

Neither prophetic preaching nor scribal preaching can demand our unquestioning assent. Both must be discerned by the body of believers as to their truthfulness and usefulness for the church. Do prophetic preachers sometimes disagree with each other? Yes, but I would claim that their disagreements are no more frequent or diverse than the disagreements among scribal preachers. The fact that prophets sometimes disagree with each other should be no more embarrassing or problematic for the church than the fact that scribes disagree with each other. Disagreement no more calls into question the legitimacy of prophetic preaching than it does scribal preaching.

The Bible is a living book through which God continues to speak a new Word to every generation. It cannot be given a final, correct interpretation—by prophet or by scribe. Therefore, authority always comes back to the ongoing discernment of the body of believers. The church listens to its preachers, whether they are scribes or prophets, and it leaves aside what is not useful and holds fast to what is good. It tests the prophets (and the scribes) with Scripture and reason and experience; it perceives whether the word spoken is self-serving or Christ-serving. The same Spirit that inspires the prophet inspires the church as a whole, and so the Spirit will lead us into all truth.

Recent homiletical theory has called into question preaching that assumes the speaker has special authority.[2] The preacher is separated from the congregation by possessing specialized knowledge and training, or superior wisdom and spiritual experience. Thus, the sermon becomes a conveyor of information or truth from a hierarchical authority. The congregation may retain a discerning role, but the overall effect is to make the congregation a passive listener, spiritually inferior to the preacher. Many going into pastoral ministry today balk at such a model of preaching, and our society in general is leery of claims to special authority—especially in the realm of religion.

At first it may appear that prophetic preaching is the very epitome of a hierarchical model in which truth is imposed downward from an authority figure. After all, it is a style that preaches "with authority." But the prophetic preaching modeled for us by Jesus and described by Paul is significantly different from traditional hierarchical preaching. First of all, as Paul notes, speaking prophetically is a gift exercised broadly in the church, by several people in every little congregation. It is never envisioned as an office belonging exclusively to ordained clergy or professionally trained personnel. In fact, the most effective sermons I have heard, in which the listeners were fully engaged and moved, were generally preached by laypersons who spoke directly and honestly from their own experience of God's involvement in life. Prophetic preaching urges us to open up the pulpit, or the worship service in general, to the inspired words of encouragement and challenge which come from the congregation. The tradition of many churches is to have the sermon at the end of the worship service—a sort of spiritual climax that emphasizes the superior nature of the clergyperson's sermon—to be followed quickly by a hymn and benediction. But prophetic preaching perhaps works better when the sermon is in the midst of the worship service, allowing the congregation an opportunity to respond individually and share their own inspired word.

From the last chapter we saw that Jesus' speaking was mostly dialogical, even when teaching in the synagogue. Crowds gathered to hear him because he had first engaged them one on one. Scribes, as well as those without special training, questioned and debated with him. Jesus spoke with a direct and immediate authority that astounded his listeners, but it did not cause them to become passive or uninvolved. If anything, his style sparked more discussion and participation.

In addition, the forms of speech Jesus used—metaphorical sayings and parables—invited listeners to interpret for themselves, draw their own conclusions, and experience the kingdom on a personal level. This is the opposite of giving answers. Rather, Jesus enabled his listeners to, in effect, become their own prophets. The paradox is surprising: his astonishing prophetic authority resulted in an egalitarian experience of God's reign among us. Prophetic preaching, as practiced by Jesus, is far less hierarchical than the professional information-based approach modeled by the scribes.

All this being said, it is still true that prophetic preaching necessitates the preacher assuming the authority to speak for God. Prophetic preaching is not arrogant authority; it is selfless and must accord others equal respect; but it embraces the authority of God's inspiration nonetheless. Those homiletical practitioners who would like to eliminate authority from the pulpit altogether are, I think, misguided. Such a goal is neither possible nor desirable. No group can function, the church included, without some individuals assuming initiative, and as soon as one initiates any word or action, that person is exercising authority. Preaching is an act of initiative. It does not matter whether the preacher is being directive, demanding certain behavior, or is facilitating a mutual discussion: either way the preacher is exercising initiative and therefore authority. Ironically, the better facilitator the preacher is, the more the congregation recognizes the authority deriving from that skill and initiative. Authority becomes damaging to the church when it is exercised selfishly or in a way that diminishes the gifts, discernment, or equal value of others in the church.

So the question is not whether preaching ought to speak with authority. The question is: What is the purpose of preaching? Is it to make the congregation more biblically knowledgeable? If so, then preachers need exegetical authority. Is it to facilitate group sharing of spiritual experiences? Then preachers need group facilitator authority. Is it to nurture ongoing faith in God? Then preachers need pastoral authority. Is it to enable conversion and transformation? Then preachers need prophetic authority. I believe that preaching includes all of these purposes, but that the most difficult of all (and thus, the most needed) is enabling spiritual transformation.

Two more objections to using Jesus as a model for prophetic preaching need to be addressed, and both have to do with the unique circumstances of Jesus' preaching context. Jesus' preaching was in sharp contrast to that of the scribes perhaps primarily because of his eschatological message: the kingdom of God is at hand. In other words, Jesus was using the future as the source of his inspiration, and the scribes were using the past (Scripture and tradition). What ought to be our orientation today? Is the kingdom of God still breaking into our world at the present moment, demanding new authoritative speech from those who speak for God? Or is God's crucial work already accomplished in the life, death, and resurrection of Jesus so that the primary focus of preaching today should be on what happened in the past?

Clearly, as Christians, we see the ministry of Jesus Christ as the ultimate revelation of the meaning and direction of history, and so we will always go back to his ministry, death, and resurrection for our direction and inspiration. However, one could argue that Jesus had a similar orientation to what God had done in the past. Certainly the Torah was Jesus' touchstone for determining the will of God and the ultimate meaning of the kingdom of God. But this rootedness in Israel's salvation history did not keep Jesus from declaring what God was doing now, and neither should our rootedness in Jesus' salvation history keep us from declaring what God is doing now. The kingdom of God is no farther away today than it was at the time of Jesus. The question is not, "Is the kingdom of God at hand?" but, "Do we personally experience and believe that the kingdom of God is at hand?" If we have not caught Jesus' eschatological vision, then, no, we cannot preach like Jesus. But if by God's grace we *have* seen the signs of God's invasion, then the possibility of preaching like Jesus remains open. The kingdom is no more hidden today than it was in Jesus' day, but Jesus dared to declare its presence anyway and call people to radical choices. So may we.

The final objection is practical rather than theological. Jesus was an itinerant preacher. His audience changed from day to day, as did the settings in which he taught and preached. Most modern preachers, however, preach to the same people Sunday after Sunday, and we do it within the same space and worship context. Since our context for preaching is so radically different from that of Jesus', to what extent can we actually use his approach to preaching as a model for our own?

Jesus' preaching was concentrated into a brief period of

time and probably repeated in every new location. Such preaching will almost inevitably be more sharp, more radical, more brilliant than that of the preacher who has to prepare a new sermon for the same people every Sunday for twenty years. If our goal is to imitate Jesus in every detail and achieve the same effect, it will not happen. I propose a goal that is more modest yet still bold: to recover for our time the transforming power of prophetic preaching that Jesus (along with John the Baptist) recovered for his own time, an empowering style of speech that influenced at least three generations of preachers in the early church.[3] The precise limitations of using Jesus as a model for prophetic preaching can be discerned only through the attempt.

And he said to them, "Therefore every scribe who has been trained for the kingdom of heaven is like the master of a household who brings out of his treasure what is new and what is old."
—Matthew 13:52

CHAPTER 6

Preaching Like Jesus

Only once is it recorded that Jesus based a sermon on a Scripture lesson (Luke 4:16-27). Otherwise, Jesus' approach to preaching was thematic rather than expository. So the first thing we may learn from Jesus is that prophetic preaching is more naturally based on biblical themes rather than explaining biblical texts.

Even among non-liturgical churches, the emphasis today in many denominations is on lectionary preaching. The lectionary is a three-year cycle of Scripture readings for each Sunday of the year. Each Sunday includes a reading from the Old Testament, the Psalms, the Gospels, and the Epistles. Preaching from the lectionary has advantages: coverage of much of the Bible, as well as the discipline of having to interpret and preach texts that may not be among one's favorites. But lectionary preaching also has disadvantages. Much of the Bible is *not* covered, and one is prevented from preaching a series of sermons on a particular theme or choosing texts that address the current needs of the congregation. A more subtle problem is the way lectionary readings break up the narrative unity of biblical books and atomize texts. Gospel readings are based on a single pericope, an isolated paragraph, fostering sermons that are narrowly focused on a particle of the larger story. The message we need to deliver to our congregations cannot always be captured by a single snapshot of Scripture. Preaching by pericope restricts the range and application of the sermon, and it invites spending the main energy of the sermon on textual archaeology—exegesis and explanation. The lectionary is a good discipline for beginning preachers and for those who maintain a scribal approach to preaching, but it is not as well suited to prophetic preaching. Prophets would probably do better to use the Bible more freely, broadly, and thematically.

In most churches, tradition dictates that a Scripture lesson be read some time before the sermon and that the sermon be based primarily on that one passage (or a combination of passages from the lectionary). This convention tends to place the sermon into an expository straightjacket. It sets up an expectation that the sermon will "be about" the passage just read. This expectation can be avoided by simply incorporating Scriptures into the sermon itself where they can be used more organically and creatively. The sermon could be punctuated with short quotes from different books of the Bible, or within the sermon the preacher might read (or recite) a longer biblical passage or story. The point is, sermons do not need to be inspired Bible lectures on particular pericopes. Much of the preaching in the first several centuries of the church was thematic or doctrinal rather than expository, which resulted in sermons ranging all over Scripture rather than focused on one passage.[1] Thematic preaching is less historical-critical (historically analyzing the pieces) and more canonical-critical (perceiving how the voices of Scripture are in dialogue together). Thematic preaching avoids the pitfall of not seeing the forest for the trees.

From this it follows that prophetic preaching spends only minimal time on exegesis (during the sermon, that is; *not* during the preparation!). Exegesis of Scripture is a completely cognitive activity, and as such it tends to move the congregation away from experiencing an encounter with God (or with Scripture, for that matter). I delight in teaching and explaining Scripture, but I have come to believe this is more helpfully accomplished in an educational setting rather than in worship. This way the sermon can focus on experiencing Scripture and God, and the Christian education classes can focus on literary and historical-critical background issues in the text. I, along with many pastors, am alarmed at the shocking biblical illiteracy even among those who attend church regularly. So I am tempted to turn my sermons into Bible lectures. But I resist, because many people in the congregation are not and never will be literary or historical learners, and besides, biblical knowledge does not convert us or save us. It educates our faith but does not produce faith. It informs us but does not transform us. The former is certainly important, but it is the latter that is essential.

Nevertheless, Bible teaching must not be neglected. If a congregation does not have a strong educational ministry that is nurturing children and informing adults, then the preacher will be compelled to be more didactic in the sermon. A didactic approach, however, does not need to be a historical-critical approach (an approach which is good for classroom knowledge but severely limited for spiritual learning). In the early church, one of the most popular exegetical approaches was to use allegorical interpretation. Modern exegetes frown on this approach since it allegorizes passages that are not allegorical, and its symbolic interpretations seem to be arbitrary. However, the allegorical method, properly understood and used, is a powerfully prophetic interpretive tool, and all good preachers make use of it.

Whenever preachers interpret a text, they need to find modern situations that in some way parallel those of the text. This is a form of allegorizing because we are viewing some items in the Scripture as symbolic for some items in our life. We do not need to assume that the biblical authors intended such applications (as ancient allegorists apparently did) for such symbolic, nonhistorical interpretations to be legitimate. If we are to make the text meaningful for our situation, we must make this symbolic connection between items in the text and items in our life.

We can press the allegorical method even further by looking for a "spiritual meaning" in the text. Rather than linking items in the text with items from the present, this approach looks for timeless spiritual meanings behind each of the characters, objects, and actions in the text. Again, this is not a historical understanding of the text. In most cases it is unlikely that the original author consciously intended deeper spiritual meanings behind the characters, objects, and actions. On the other hand, one could argue that deeper spiritual meanings are always present *unconsciously* to the original author. But whether these spiritual meanings come from the author or not, the community of faith is still justified in discovering such meanings, because it was this process which turned scripture into Scripture.

For instance, most historical-critical exegetes believe that the Song of Solomon was originally a collection of secular love songs between a man and a woman, and scholars unanimously reject the idea that the Song of Solomon was meant to be an allegory of God's love. However, it was not as a collection of secular love songs that the Song of Solomon came into widespread use by synagogue and church. Rather, the synagogue and the church interpreted this book allegorically as spiritual love songs between God and the believer. Early rabbis went so far as to forbid interpreting it historically: "He who trills his voice in the chanting of the Song of Songs in the banquet-halls and treats it as a secular song, has no share in the world to come" (Tosefta Sanhedrin 12.10). Allegorical interpretation certainly played an important role in the eventual canonization of the Song of Solomon as Scripture, and so it can be argued that *as a canonical book of Scripture*, the Song of Solomon should be interpreted spiritually, even though this is not its original, historical meaning.

Looking for the inner spiritual meaning of a Scripture

text was the normal way of interpreting in the early church. This is what gave texts a present meaning for the believing community. And since the method was so widespread and assumed, we should be cautious in asserting that biblical authors did not intend underlying spiritual meanings. Nevertheless, every book of the Bible is in the Bible only because the believing community experienced those books as being capable of continuous spiritual meaning, regardless of the original intent of the authors.

The authors of the Gospels make frequent use of the allegorical method. Matthew in particular interprets all kinds of Old Testament texts as symbolically referring to Jesus even though their historical meaning is quite different (e.g., Matt. 1:22-23: 2:17-18, 23). As we have already seen, the Gospel writers allegorized the parable of the soils. Even though their interpretation is unlikely to have been the meaning Jesus intended, it is still a spiritually powerful and truthful interpretation of Jesus' parable. To see the birds and thorns and scorching sun as symbols of those things in our lives that can rob us of faith is a needed lesson, regardless of whether that

Scribal Preaching	Prophetic Preaching
teach	proclaim
mind	soul
thinking	feeling
describe	enact
explain	experience
intellectual	inspired
inform	transform
letter	Spirit
old word	new word
read	recite
expository	thematic
historical	spiritual
atomistic	canonical
past orientation	present-future orientation
institutional credentials	faith and character credentials

is the historical meaning of the parable. Indeed, some of Jesus' parables probably continued to be remembered and retold in the early church because of the useful allegorical interpretations added later (e.g., Matt. 13:36-43).

I have already mentioned that Jesus' parables functioned as parables, not as allegories, and that this is an important point as we seek to model our preaching on his. But this does not mean that we, as preachers, ought not to allegorize. On the contrary, when exegeting a text, this is a spiritually more helpful and engaging method than the historical-critical method. As scribes we need to be thoroughly familiar with the meanings revealed through historical and literary analysis of a text, but as preachers we need to present to our congregations interpretations which have spiritual and transformative meanings. The allegorical method can be a creative, prophetic tool to this end.

Prophetic preaching certainly can be rational, abstract, and directive (Paul's letters are particularly powerful examples of this type of prophetic preaching), but Jesus' example invites us to limit ideas and speak in images instead. Given the fact that our culture is moving away from written information and toward visual communication, we would do well to focus on the use of images in our preaching. When preparing a sermon, remove as many abstract statements as possible and replace them with visual illustrations or metaphors. For instance, I could say to my congregation, "In order to give your life to God you must let go of your ego, ambitions, accomplishments, as well as your failures," or I could say, "The kingdom of God is like a nudist colony—if you want to get in you have to take everything off." Which communicates more? Which is more memorable? Which invites participation and reflection? Images speak louder than abstractions. They more readily create an experience because of their parallel to life situations, and they invite interpretation that makes the listener an equal participant in the quest of the sermon. Besides, the more sparingly we speak in ideas, the more powerful they become.

Prophetic preaching possesses an important characteristic that we have not yet examined: the ability to see deeply into individuals and to bring to the light what hearers have kept hidden. On one occasion, Jesus' prophetic status is questioned because of his apparent ignorance of an individual's spiritual condition: "If this man were a prophet, he would have known who and what kind of woman this is who is touching him—that she is a sinner" (Luke 7:39). But not only does Jesus know the woman's true condition, but he also apparently knows what his critic is thinking! In fact, Luke explicitly tells us that on two other occasions Jesus knew what others were secretly thinking (6:8; 11:17). This ability is part of what makes a person a prophet: knowing what is hidden inside others' psyches and addressing them accordingly.

We see this ability again in the story of Zacchaeus (Luke 19:1-10). Zacchaeus is apparently unknown to Jesus, and yet when Jesus sees him in a tree, he immediately "sizes up" the small man, invites himself to Zacchaeus' home, and facilitates his conversion to a radically new way of life. The assumption is that Jesus, possessing the gifts of a prophet, is able to see what makes others "spiritually tick," and thus can effectively motivate them. Similarly, the Gospel writers seem to assume that Jesus picks his disciples, even if he has not met them before, through an extraordinary spiritual intuition (e.g., Mark 1:16-20).

Clearly such an ability would enable one's preaching to be far more compelling and transformative. The prophetic preacher sees into the hearers, understanding their condition and spiritual needs, and openly addresses what may be hidden from the hearers themselves.

But isn't this a supernatural ability given only to the very few? Is it realistic to expect that modern preachers may exercise this prophetic gift in their preaching? In Paul's experience, this gift was available in every little house-church: "But if all prophesy, an unbeliever or outsider who enters is reproved by all and called to account by all. After the secrets of the unbeliever's heart are disclosed, that person will bow down before God and worship him, declaring, 'God is really among you'" (1 Cor. 14:24-25). The prophetic ability to see the spiritual condition of others (and oneself), and to courageously bring our shadows into the light, is an ability more available to us than we have dared to practice. Scribal preaching is safe preaching: it speaks about things "out there." But prophetic preaching has the spiritual nerve to be personal, vulnerable, and expose what we are all hiding. This is what makes prophetic preaching transformative. It is honest and revealing, focusing on who we are before God in this moment.

When watching a TV news anchorperson, how often is the person looking down at notes rather than into the camera? When listening to a professional storyteller, how often is the person reading out of a book or from a manuscript rather than looking at you as the story is told? Eye contact is the energy of verbal communication, and so prophetic preaching is best done without a manuscript or notes.

That Jesus preached without notes is beside the point (as far as we know, no rabbis or teachers used notes; Jesus' culture was predominantly oral). I raise the issue of preaching without notes simply because it is such a good idea. I have not used notes in preaching for the past seven years, and I hope I never will again. Not only is eye contact established throughout the sermon, but the voice becomes more conversational and natural, and the entire body is freed up to express itself. Preaching without notes gives the sermon immediacy, intimacy, and a greater sense of importance and honesty.

Preaching without notes can be accomplished in two different ways: memorizing or extemporizing. I recommend a combination of both. Preachers need to develop their own methods that work best for them. In my own case, I write out my sermons word-for-word. Then, the night before I preach, I read through the sermon twice out loud. Then I go to bed. Sleeping seems to aid my memory, because when I wake up in the morning the sermon is fairly firm in my mind. I practice it one more time without the manuscript, and then I go to church and preach it. I never take the manuscript into the pulpit where I might be tempted to fall back on it. Do I ever forget a part of the sermon? On rare occasions, but the immediacy and eye contact make accidental omissions worthwhile. Do I ever get stuck, not knowing what to say next? Not really, because the flow of the sermon allows me to extemporize whenever I want to. (In order to keep a record for my file, I always take the original manuscript and write in the margins all the things I said during the sermon which I had not originally planned to say.)

Memorizing sermons takes practice. I spent about a year slowly weaning myself off manuscripts and then off notes. In the process, I decided to memorize and recite all of my Scriptures as well. This has given me dramatic new insights into the Scriptures, as well as making the Scripture more of a living word for my congregation. Many excellent preachers read their sermons and Scriptures, but I have come to a different conclusion: scribes read, prophets speak.

Key to Jesus' prophetic preaching were his kingdom-revealing acts: healings, exorcisms, and prophetic signs. Even his itinerancy was a symbolic way of preaching—demonstrating utter trust in God and freedom from possessions. Those who would preach like Jesus must likewise live out their message and reveal the reality of God's reign.

The Gospels report that Jesus healed people of physical illnesses, but behind the physical healings was a spiritual healing: the forgiveness of sins and the assurance that God, not chaos, is in control. The modern preacher may or may not have a gift for bringing physical healing to people, but if the preacher can make real the presence and forgiveness of God, we should not be surprised if physical benefits also result. Our worldview may or may not allow for the literal existence of interfering demons, but the prophetic preacher should certainly be in the business of casting out the shame, alienation, and fear that possess and destroy the personalities of those in our congregations.

Healing can be symbolized, and therefore made more real, through the use of rituals such as anointing with oil. As the Letter of James says, "Are any among you sick? They should call for the elders of the church and have them pray over them, anointing them with oil in the name of the Lord. The prayer of faith will save the sick, and the Lord will raise them up; and anyone who has committed sins will be forgiven" (5:14-15). Oil was used as a healing agent in the ancient world; so when the church applied oil on a believer, accompanied by prayer, it was symbolizing physical healing as well as the spiritual healing (forgiveness) which undergirds it. Such rituals ought to continue to be used by the preacher and the church, not as a tradition, but as a symbol of a present reality.

Communion is a ritual the church continues to practice, deriving from a symbolic act originating with Jesus. It is my observation, however, that communion is sometimes practiced as a scribal tradition rather than as a true enactment of a spiritual reality. Instead of little cups and wafers, consider using big loaves of bread and wineglasses. Instead of sitting in the pew or standing in line, lead the congregation outside to sit on the green grass, reenacting the feeding of the multitude. I am not advocating innovation for its own sake (I am put off by supposedly creative rituals that are ultimately trite or coercive); rather, I am urging that our fundamental rituals become actual spiritual enactments in the minds and hearts of the people.

In addition to making prophetic use of the traditional rituals of the church, prophetic preachers need to follow Jesus' example by enacting what they are preaching. Is it a sermon about our need to step away from work for spiritual rest? Take off your shoes and sit on a stool while you preach this. Is it a sermon warning the congregation about impressing others by how we look and making judgments based on outward appearances? Wear an old T-shirt while you preach this. Is it a sermon about our need to love our future neighbors by not ruining the environment? Ride a bike to church that Sunday. You've heard it before: practice what you preach. This is the essence of prophetic preaching, and it goes beyond symbolic actions in the pulpit to how we live each day. Demonstrate freedom from status-seeking by living in a small house and driving an old car. Enact God's boundary-breaking kingdom by living in an integrated neighborhood with integrated schools. Practice God's grace by inviting your most vocal critic home for dinner. As Francis of Assisi said: Preach at all times. If necessary, use words.

The kingdom of God is like dandelions growing in the front yard of a suburban home. "What will our neighbors think!" exclaimed the young couple as they opened their bedroom curtains. The husband immediately went to the Ace Hardware store to pick up a bag of Scott's Weed Killer while his wife got down on her hands and knees and began pulling the dandelions out one by one. By the end of the morning they had irradicated all of the dandelions and had spread the weed killer over the entire lawn. Relieved, they retired to their comfortable home.

But the next Saturday morning, when they pulled back their bedroom curtains, the dandelions were back—dozens of them. Quickly, before their neighbors might notice, they raced outside and once again pulled them all up and spread another layer of weed killer. Again they felt relief.

But the following Saturday morning, when they pulled back their curtains, they were shocked to see even more dandelions—scores of them. The husband rushed outside, started up the lawn mower, and mowed them all down.

And yet, the next Saturday morning, when they pulled back their bedroom curtains, they saw to their horror hundreds of dandelions everywhere. Defeated, the couple closed the curtains and laid back in bed. Later they heard their children wake up and go outside, and within a few minutes they heard the noise of their return and the sound of kitchen cabinets opening and shutting, and glassware tinkling. A moment later there was a knock on their bedroom door, and in came a six-year-old boy and his four-year-old sister who was holding a vase filled with dandelions. "Look, Mom and Dad, flowers!" exclaimed the girl. "Aren't they beautiful?" smiled the boy. "They're for you."

CHAPTER 7

Creating New Parables

The backbone of Jesus' preaching was his parables, so the preacher who is using Jesus as a model will naturally give this form of speaking close attention. Most preachers, when preaching on one of Jesus' parables, take one of the following approaches: (1) analyze the characters, setting, and structure of the parable in order to explain its meaning; (2) paraphrase the parable, emphasizing the most interesting aspects of the story; or (3) retell the parable in a modern setting with modern characters.

The first approach is a strictly scribal approach, and it misunderstands and misuses the parable by attempting to break it down into ideas. The second approach respects the parable form but is still focused on uncovering a historical understanding. The third approach is the most creative of the three, and may succeed in enabling hearers to experience the parable, but it is merely mimicking Jesus rather than doing what Jesus did. Most often the congregation sees through imitations too readily, identifying and latching on to the original—an original that has already lost its edge by being too familiar and tamed through conventional interpretation. The best way, perhaps the only true way, to interpret a parable is to tell a new parable.[1]

If we are to speak prophetically as Jesus spoke, then we must be inspired by God to speak a new word to our congregations that enables them to perceive and experience what God is doing now. We cannot simply mimic or retell Jesus' parables; we must create new parables that will facilitate a similar revealing of God's reality.

> An oil tanker ran aground on a reef. Millions of barrels of crude oil poured out of the shattered hull into the ocean. Soon the oil spill lapped up on the beaches, covering rocks and sand, seals and birds with a thick layer of black ooze.
>
> The oil company desperately tried to contain the spill, but it was too late. Day after day more crude covered the beaches. The oil company sent specialists to the beaches with solvents and vacuums, and hordes of environmentalists came to the scene with towels and brushes. They worked long hours for many days, scrubbing the rocks and rescuing the animals, but as soon as they finished a stretch of beach, another wave of black oil would sweep over it all again. After several weeks the oil company ran out of money to clean the beaches, and the volunteers became victims of compassion fatigue, and so they all finally gave up and left.
>
> But the ocean continued lapping on the beaches, wave after wave, year after year. Slowly, gently, invisibly, the ocean massaged each rock, each pebble, and each grain of sand, until all the crude was cleaned away. God's kingdom is like this.

In order to create new parables in the spirit of Jesus, we should first do some scribal analysis of how Jesus' parables are constructed, how they differ from each other, and identify their basic themes. To simplify the task, I will focus only on those parables that appear to be explicitly about the kingdom of God. For those parables that appear in more than one Gospel, I will consider only one version. They are:

The soils	Mark 4:3-9
The seed growing secretly	Mark 4:26-29
The mustard seed	Mark 4:30-32

The weeds in the wheat	Matt. 13:24-30
The yeast	Matt. 13:33
The hidden treasure	Matt. 13:44
The pearl	Matt. 13:45-46
The net	Matt. 13:47-48
The day laborers	Matt. 20:1-16
The ten bridesmaids	Matt. 25:1-13
The talents	Matt. 25:14-30
The sheep and the goats	Matt. 25:31-46
The great dinner	Luke 14:16-24
The rich man and Lazarus	Luke 16:19-31
The Pharisee and the tax collector	Luke 18:10-14

Within this body of parables, most can be placed into the broad thematic category of *the boundaries of the kingdom of God* (or: who's in, who's out). These parables include: the net, the ten bridesmaids, the sheep and the goats, the talents, the great dinner, the rich man and Lazarus, and the Pharisee and the tax collector. All of these parables involve some sort of separation of those who are ultimately "in" from those who are ultimately "out." In all of them, except the net, the ultimate division comes as a surprise: those who are out do not expect to be left out (and in most cases those who are in do not expect to be in). Indeed, the listener of the parable is usually sympathetic to those left out and feels it is not only shocking but perhaps even unjust. Why should the man with one talent have it taken away when all he was doing was being prudent? Why should half the bridesmaids be left out just because they weren't prepared for an unexpectedly long wait?

Three of these parables heighten the in/out theme by totally reversing the initial positions of the characters: the rich man is left out of heaven while the destitute Lazarus receives it; the pious Pharisee is unforgiven while the despicable tax collector is justified; the invited friends become disinvited while strangers and panhandlers get the feast. Over-interpretation of these parables has taken away much of their sting, but certainly for the original hearers all of these reversals would have seemed utterly shocking and unfair. Another parable that emphasizes unexpected unfairness and a sort of reversal is the parable of the day laborers. It differs from the in/out parables by the fact that everyone receives the same (though unexpected) fortune.

At the risk of minimizing the meaning of these parables, it appears that one of Jesus' main parabolic themes was the unexpectedness of who is part of God's kingdom and who is not. The boundaries of God's kingdom are not determined by piety, respectability, or playing it safe. Rather, those who have nothing to lose, or act as though they have nothing to lose, become a part of God's kingdom.

Two parables, with an entirely different structure, make a similar point. These are the parables of the hidden treasure and the pearl. Unlike the in/out parables, there is no separation and no reversal. Also, these two parables contain just a single character. The simplicity of these two parables focuses our attention on the decision and action of the character. Everything hangs on this decision, and in both parables we see the character give up literally everything in order to obtain that which is greater. The effect is to startle the listener, not with the character's ultimate fortune, but with the enormity of the sacrifice to obtain it. The listener is implicitly challenged to do the same. The parable of the talents, although it differs by involving separation of characters, makes the same point: one must risk all to enter God's reign. The parables of the hidden treasure and pearl, perhaps along with the talents, belong in a category related to kingdom boundaries: *the need to risk or lose all to enter the kingdom.*

The remaining kingdom parables are quite different from those we have considered above. These do not have human characters as their central actors. Instead, the central activity is performed by something from nature. In all but one of the parables this central actor is seed (the soils, the seed growing secretly, the mustard seed, the weeds in the wheat), and in the other it is yeast. In all of these parables the central activity is growth. Clearly, these parables belong together in their own category: *the growth of the kingdom.*[2]

These parables, like virtually all of the in/out parables, have surprising endings. A tiny mustard seed unexpectedly becomes an enormous plant, a seed planted in the ground mysteriously becomes a head of grain without any human help, a hidden ingredient makes the bread rise, and after repeated failures some seed produces a harvest that more than makes up for losses. The parable of the weeds in the wheat at first appears to be the oddball in this bunch. It seems to be a separation parable about the kingdom's boundaries (and so it was interpreted by Matthew). But if we leave off Matthew's allegorical explanation, it may be a parable about how the kingdom grows despite what appear to be disastrous problems (thus making it similar to the parable of the soils).

Another characteristic these parables have in common is a lack of human involvement. The reign of God grows almost despite human beings. It is hidden, mysterious, tiny, but persistent. It will not fail. And when it comes to its ultimate fruition, then human beings will enjoy all its fruits.

If we are going to preach about God's kingdom with an understanding and experience consistent with Jesus', then we will likely create metaphorical narratives that reveal the kingdom's growth in our world, its shocking boundaries, and the total commitment and risk it requires to be a part of it. When creating parables in the spirit of Jesus, they should use everyday images, realistic situations, and remain open-ended for the listener's interpretation and involvement. This does not mean that the preacher may not follow up the parable with clear and direct pronouncements (Jesus does so in the Gospels). Congregations soon grow weary of sermons that float around like beautiful but vague clouds. But what is to be avoided is explanation of the parable. This would be as counterproductive as explaining a joke one has used in the sermon.

The local church had been broken into several times. The first time some pictures of Jesus that had been hanging on the walls were stolen. The second time quite a few books from the library were taken. The third time those little Heifer Project banks, full of nickels and dimes, were swiped from the church office.

Neither the congregation nor the police had any idea who was breaking in. But the police did point out that the locks on the building were old and easily picked. Another problem was the disbursement of keys. Over the years keys had been given out to a wide variety of church members, many of whom no longer attended, and it was now impossible to tell who might have access to a key.

So the trustees decided it was time to change the locks and keep track of the new keys more carefully. They called the best locksmith in town who came out and installed an advanced security system. Instead of regular locks with keys, he installed those locks that require a special magnetic card to open, and on all the windows he installed a silent alarm. When he was done, he presented the pastor and trustees with the needed magnetic cards.

The next day was Sunday, and as people began arriving for church, the trustees went to the front door and inserted one of the cards. Nothing happened. They went through all the cards, including the pastor's, and tried every door, but none of the locks would open. In the meantime the parking lot was filling up with cars, and people were wondering what was going on. One of the trustees had a cell phone and called the locksmith shop, but it wasn't open on Sunday and no one answered. They tried a few other locksmiths, but with the same result. By now two hundred people had arrived and were standing around outside the church. The pastor apologized to everyone for the fiasco and suggested they all go home.

After everyone had left, the pastor stood outside the church wondering what to do. Inside, on the desk in his study, were the names and addresses of several families he needed to visit that day. He walked around the building trying to find a way in. Then he saw a small basement window, and through the pane a little lever that would open the window. He considered the cost of the pane of glass and decided he would cover it out of his own pocket. So he got down on the ground and with the heel of his shoe kicked in the glass. He then reached in and unlocked the window. Then he opened the window and, feet first, began squirming his way through.

But there were two things he had not reckoned on: the window was just a little bit smaller than his body, and he had forgotten that all the windows had a silent alarm. Within three minutes a squad car pulled into the parking lot, lights flashing, and two officers jumped out, unsnapping their holsters. They apprehended the pastor who was stuck in the basement window. He said he was the pastor and that he was just trying to get into his church. They said, "Sure," and took him away for questioning.

That night the church was broken into again. This time they took the communion set.[3]

Creating parables that function like Jesus' parables is difficult, and the pitfalls are many. Perhaps the most common is creating a paraphrase rather than a parable. Particularly when just one of Jesus' parables is used as a model, it is easy to fall into simply updating the characters and situation. A creative twist on the paraphrase approach, which can be highly effective, is to change the direction of one of Jesus' parables, and play with the theological implications. For instance, in the parable of the talents, what if the first two servants had risked all of their master's money and lost it (while the third servant had prudently saved his one talent by burying it)? How would the master have reacted then? The parable retains its original theme while becoming shocking once again if the master still congratulates the first two servants and dismisses the third.

Or another imaginative approach is to extend the original

story and explore further questions. What if the good Samaritan, after helping the wounded man, returned later to the inn to discover that the man had run up an incredible and frivolous bill which the Samaritan was obliged to pay? And what if, after being taken advantage of, the Samaritan comes across another wounded man—what will he do? Playing with Jesus' parables in this way saves a paraphrase from predictability.

Another negative tendency is to create allegories rather than parables. Allegories are not bad, but they do not function the way Jesus' parables do and they are less challenging to the hearer. Allegory results from being too doctrinal and idea-oriented. Trust the story to work as a story. Don't worry if the individual parts don't have meaning.

Also avoid creating conventional morality tales that simply reinforce the values we already have and which "feel good." None of Jesus' parables, and virtually none of his sayings, were of a conventional, feel-good variety. The reign of God among us is fundamentally against the status quo we humans create, and it demands choices of the most radical kind. The prophetic preacher will reject from consideration all those predictable, insipid, tear-jerking stories one finds in popular book collections and on the Internet.

Perhaps most difficult is creating a parable that is shocking yet still realistic. The urge to move into fantasy is strong. New Testament scholar John Dominic Crossan rightly observes that "unexpected action must be spelled out in enough detail to make it convincing, or it will be rejected out of hand."[4] Jesus' artistic ability shines through most brilliantly when one considers the successful ways he created realistic double reversals (insiders out, outsiders in). One should note, though, that Jesus sometimes accomplished this by appealing to an eschatological judgment—something harder to do in a convincing way in our culture.

When creating a parable in which the insiders are left outside, it is natural to make the insiders unsympathetic, and instead to lodge our sympathies with the previous outsiders who are now in. But this destroys the shock and offense of the parable. Jesus' double reversal parables are particularly disturbing precisely because our sympathies are with those who are ultimately left outside. To be true to Jesus' intention and spirit, our parable must function in the same way.

A more subtle pitfall is creating a literary parable rather than an oral one. If the parable is going to be preached, then it should use the same forms of speech that a joke would use. Take out the complex grammar and distinctive words that call attention to themselves when spoken. Take out all details or descriptions which are either unneeded or might bore the listener. And, as much as possible, replace abstractions, thoughts, and feelings with objects and actions.

Finally, a parable must be understandable as well as open-ended. Parables have multiple meanings, but they cannot be vague or mean whatever the hearer wants them to mean. When Jesus taught in parables, he hads a clear intent in mind. At the very least, he wanted to convey a particular understanding and experience of God's reality subversively entering our world. If the listener experienced something else, or was unmoved to become a disciple, then Jesus' parables failed. A parable proclaims as well as teases, so when one or more parables are incorporated into a sermon their overall effect must be to aid the proclamation.

Once there was a good Mennonite.[5] He refused to go to war, shared his possessions with the poor, lived an environmentally sustainable lifestyle, and was active in his church.

One day he died and immediately found himself before a gate covered with rubies, emeralds, and diamonds. Two massive golden doors swung open and inside stood Menno Simons, beaming with sublime joy. "Welcome to heaven!" he exclaimed. "I've been waiting all your life for you to get here and join me. Come on in!"

The Mennonite stepped in and with great satisfaction said to himself, "I did it! All that simple living and going to Relief Sales paid off!"

Menno Simons asked, "Would you like to have a tour of heaven?" The man answered, "I'd love to." So Menno Simons took him down streets paved with gold and lined by palaces greater than the Taj Mahal. They passed a park with a great rainbow and a waterfall so magnificent it made Niagara Falls look like a dripping spigot. Finally, at the end of one street they came to the finest mansion of all. "This house is yours," said Menno Simons.

They turned up the sidewalk and entered the mansion. It had crystal chandeliers in every room, fourteen bathrooms, a living room with a giant hot tub, and a dining room the size of a football field. "Would you like something to eat?" asked Menno Simons. "Sure, that would be great," said the man. Menno Simons ducked into the kitchen and a few minutes later came out with two peanut butter and jelly sandwiches on an ivory platter. They sat down at the huge dining room table and munched on their sandwiches.

After a while the man asked, "Menno, what's there to do up here in heaven? What kind of entertainment do you have?" Menno thought for a moment and said, "Well, one thing that's pretty fun is a telescope that looks down into hell. You can see everything going on down there. You want to take a look?" "Sure," said the man, "that sounds neat."

So Menno took the man outside and brought him back to the park; and there, mounted at the edge of heaven, was a long telescope pointing down into hell. Menno adjusted the focus and then invited the man to take a look.

Sure enough, there it was: hell, filled with millions upon millions upon millions of people. As the man scanned the crowd he recognized some of the people. "Oh, there's Linda Yoder. She always was a troublemaker, pushing her own agenda and gossiping about people. No surprise she's in hell. And look over there—it's Chuck Bontrager. He embezzled money from his company and shamed the whole church. . . . Well look at that—it's Pam Nofzinger. Everyone knows she had an illegitimate baby. . . . Wait a minute, I see Glen Roth. What's he doing down there? I always thought he was a decent guy. It must have been that big house he built that led to his condemnation." As the man scanned the crowd, he saw a barefoot fellow with scars on his hands. He looked vaguely familiar.

Well it must have been supper time in hell, because everybody sat down at a huge table, and on the table was fried chicken and jumbo shrimp and filet mignon, and there were mashed potatoes and gravy and sweet potatoes and mixed vegetables and fruit salad. And for dessert there was banana creme pie and chocolate cheesecake.

The man looked away from the telescope puzzled and thought for a moment. Then he turned to Menno Simons and asked, "There's something I don't understand. Down there in hell everyone is having a fantastic feast, but up here in heaven all you gave me was a peanut butter and jelly sandwich."

Menno Simons shrugged, "No use cooking for just the two of us."

CHAPTER 8

Prophetic Sermon Samples

In this chapter I present five sermons I have preached. They are not polished, literary products; rather, they are acts of verbal passion, still in the rough, containing a diverse sampling of prophetic elements. The variety here will hopefully discourage the notion that prophetic preaching follows only one form. In fact, prophetic preaching can be adapted and integrated into many styles and formats.

Each of these sermons, in its own way, was inspired by the example of Jesus' preaching. They all seek to hear God's Word for us now, concentrating on a present proclamation rather than an exposition of the past.

The first sermon is the most similar to Jesus' own style of preaching. I was consciously imitating Jesus' parables and metaphorical sayings, imagining what a sermon by Jesus might sound like if he were preaching to us today. The text here is a revision of a sermon I preached to my congregation, Peoria-North Mennonite Church, on September 18, 1994. The format and presentation were an experiment. Instead of preaching from the pulpit in the sanctuary, I sat in a chair in the basement fellowship hall with the congregation seated in concentric circles, creating a more intimate and dialogical (but peculiar) atmosphere.

Risky Business

Key Text: Luke 9:23-25, 57-62

Unless you become like a person infected with AIDS you'll never receive God's healing. Unless you become a convict, you'll never experience God's freedom. Unless you become senile, you'll never understand the truth. Unless you become an idiot, you'll never grasp God's wisdom. Unless you become like a drug addict, you'll never experience God's sobriety.

God cannot be embraced until our hands are empty and we've lost everything. We must be like the alcoholic who has lost his job, his friends, and his family before he realizes he has no control and must turn himself over to that which is greater.

Who wants to know how to become a part of God's new world? . . . Then listen carefully:

One day Mario Andretti called up his three nephews—

Jeff, John, and Jerry—and asked them to come over to his house. When they arrived he took them into his den and they all sat down on the big leather couches. Mario said to them, "Boys, I'm going to Europe for six months to race in the Formula One races, and my son Michael is coming with me. I'd like you boys to take care of my other cars while I'm gone. Jeff, I'm going to put my Indy car in your hands. Take good care of it while I'm gone. John, I'm going to give you my NASCAR. Take good care of it while I'm gone. And Jerry, I'm going to leave my dragster with you. Take care of it."

The next day Mario got on a plane and left for Europe. The nephew, Jeff, went to the Andretti garage to take a look at the Indy car. There it was: sleek and powerful. He sat in the small seat, wedging himself into the car. He started the engine—the roar was incredible and the feeling of power at his fingertips overwhelming. Filled with a passion he had never known before, he decided he must enter the Indianapolis 500 and win the race.

He lost no time making preparations—finding financial backers and putting together a pit crew. He went to the time trials and qualified for the race. Then, on Memorial Day weekend, he lined up his car on the track with all the other cars. Everyone started their engines. The blast of noise filled him with adrenaline. The pace car led them down the track and then moved aside. The race began.

Jeff tore down the track, increasing his speed to over 220 miles per hour. He could barely control the steering wheel as he passed one car after another. But then, two laps into the race, on one of the curves, his front right tire touched the wall and his car went tumbling out of control, smashing to pieces.

The next nephew, John, went to look at the NASCAR Mario had left in his care. The moment his eyes fell on that blue beauty, he knew it was his destiny to race it. Right away he began making preparations to enter the Brickyard 400.

He got the sponsors and crew he needed, and then in August he took the car to the Indianapolis Brickyard 400. He raced spectacularly, his NASCAR weaving in and out at strategic points until he took the lead. But then, with one lap to go, another car clipped him, spinning him around and sending him into the wall. The car was demolished.

The third nephew, Jerry, went to the garage to take a look at the dragster his uncle Mario put in his care. When he saw the bright red color and painted flames, he had a sudden vision of himself at Raceway Park, driving the dragster to victory.

But then he thought, "No, I better not. Uncle Mario would kill me if his car got even a scratch on it." So he carefully washed it, waxed it, put a cover over it, and kept it locked up in the garage.

Six months later Mario Andretti returned from Europe and called up his three nephews and asked them to come over. When they all arrived, he looked at each of them in disbelief and said, "What happened!"

Jeff blurted, "I'm so sorry! I don't know what I was thinking. I took your car to the Indy 500. I was going to race it for you and bring back that big trophy and put it in your hands and say, 'Thanks, Uncle!' But instead, I crashed and your car is destroyed."

Mario's frown turned into a grin. He slapped Jeff on the shoulder and said, "That took guts! You have the heart of a racer, and I'm proud of you. I'm going to buy you your own Indy car, and you're going to race again!"

John then said, "Uncle Mario, I don't know what got into me. I felt possessed. I took your car to the Brickyard 400, and I was so excited about winning and giving you all that prize money. But instead, all I can give you is this dented fender. Your car is ruined. I'm sorry."

Mario Andretti gave him a hug and said, "At least you tried. You risked everything because racing is in your blood, and I'm proud of you. You lost the Brickyard but you won in here. I'm going to buy you your own NASCAR so you can try again."

Then his nephew Jerry stepped forward with a smile of satisfaction. "Uncle Mario, unlike your other nephews, I was careful and responsible. I kept your dragster locked up and safe in the garage the whole six months. Here are the keys."

Mario looked at his nephew in puzzlement. "You never raced it?"

"Nope, I didn't want anything to happen to it."

"Jerry, where's your backbone? Where's your zeal? Where's your passion to race? You'll never be a racer, and no one will ever hear of you." And then Mario gave the dragster to Jeff.

If you play it safe, you die. If you risk everything—your comfort, your security, your possessions, your reputation, your friendships—you live. God wants all of you. Not just your head, not your lips, not your hands, not your heart, not your feet. It's all or nothing. If you've hidden a little part for yourself, then you're really controlling it all. It all belongs to God or it doesn't really belong to God at all.

Americans live in America. Russians live in Russia. Nigerians live in Nigeria. But citizens of God's nation belong nowhere and belong to no one. You are hobos for God. You own nothing, but as you move about you possess everything.

A husband and wife drove to Grand View Drive and picnicked on the bluff overlooking the Illinois River. After eating in the shade of the big trees, they strolled down the road, pointing out their favorite mansions and admiring the best views of the forest and the river below. And without spending a dime, they owned all those homes and all those views.

Any questions?

God's new world order is a way of living. One day a man attended the funeral of a friend he had known since childhood. As he stood by the casket looking at the stiff, mannequin body, he suddenly realized with terrible clarity how fragile life is.

When he got home he called up his insurance company and doubled his life insurance, health insurance, and worker compensation insurance on himself, his wife, and his children. The following day he began a rigorous diet and exercise program, and went to the doctor for blood work and chest x-rays. A couple of days later he bought a new car with dual and side airbags, antilock brakes, an alarm system, and a club on the steering wheel.

Then he moved to a gated community and put an alarm system throughout his house, motion detection lights outside, wrought iron grills on his basement windows, and a high fence around his property. He bought two Doberman pinschers and taught them to attack on command.

He took his wife and sons to karate lessons and to a pistol range several days a week until they'd become proficient at firearms and martial arts.

As a result, this man's family never suffered a serious accident, never had a break-in, and were never bothered by strangers or by neighbors.

A woman, who had attended the same funeral, was also shaken up by the realization of life's fragility. When she got home she took her son in her arms, looked deeply into his face, and told him how much she loved him. She did that every day.

When she was out driving and saw hitchhikers, she picked them up. She also started volunteering at the Salvation Army soup kitchen, and when she met a woman who was being kicked out of her apartment with nowhere to go, she invited her into her own home and helped her find a job and keep a budget. Neighbors and strangers often came to her door, and she invited them in and assisted them when she could.

She taught her son how to help others. She also taught

him how to run when being chased, how to tell a joke to defuse hostility, and how to buy a candy bar for someone who doesn't like you.

As a result, this woman was sometimes taken advantage of, and a few things disappeared from around her house. Her son wasn't always able to avoid or defuse the hostility of bullies, and she herself was once mugged.

Which of these two people, the man or the woman, is really alive? . . . Then do the same and you'll experience the dawning of God's new world.

Don't be afraid. God's new world is close by and God wants to give it to you. It's not yours because you're strong, but because you know you're weak. It's not yours because you're good, but because you know you aren't. It's not yours because you achieved it, but because you've given up.

Let go, drop every fear and every worry, every achievement and every shame, and your hands will be free to embrace God alone. You can do it because God has also let go of everything and is embracing you.

God is like a toddler collecting stones by the driveway. She picks up itty-bitty ones and big ones, brown ones and black ones, smooth ones and rough ones. She has a field day when she sees gravel! Every stone has to be picked up and possessed, because to that toddler every stone is a gem. And woe to the person who tries to take away even one!

The marriage of heaven and earth is beginning. Don't doubt it. Believe it and join the party! Pass up all other invitations. *This* is the big event!

The organ music has already begun. The sanctuary is full of flowers. The bridesmaids and groomsmen are in place. In the fellowship hall the three-tiered cake is now set up. Listen to the music swelling. The mother is rising. Look behind you—the bride is entering! It's the marriage of heaven and earth!

This next sermon is a much more familiar type of topical sermon. It begins and ends with folktale parables, but the body of the sermon is a rational discourse directed to "the insiders"—the disciples, as it were. As in most of Jesus' teaching, this sermon's use of Scripture is thematic rather than expository, and its focus is constantly on the present and on what God may be saying to us and our society now. I preached it on September 7, 1997, to my congregation, First Mennonite Church, in Indianapolis.

Recovering Our Religious Center

Key Text: John 1:1-13

According to a pygmy legend, a little boy went into the forest one day and he found a bird that sung the most beautiful song. The little boy was enchanted by the song. He held out his hand and the bird flew right to him. He brought the bird home and made a little nest for it in the corner of his hut. Then he went to his father and said, "May I have some food to feed my bird?" But the father didn't want to waste food on a mere bird, so he took the bird and wrung its neck. But when he killed the bird, he killed the song; and when he killed the song, he killed himself. And he dropped dead, completely dead, and was dead forever.

We live in a society that has killed the bird. We live in a society that does not value its song and has not even heard its song. We live in a society that has no religious center. And because it has no religious center, it has no soul, and it is not alive.

But we are a counter society, an alternative society. We are a society with a soul, a society with a religious center. And because of that we hear the song and we are *alive*.

The religious person realizes that *everything* around us is a miracle and a mysterious gift. The religious person perceives that despite all the randomness and pointless tragedy, underneath it all is a meaningfulness—that our minds, our consciousness, our highest dreams and values are all connected to the mind of God. The religious person sees that the reality beyond the realm of science is actually larger than the reality within the realm of science. In fact, we are all essentially religious. Whether we know it or not, we are religious. Even if we are atheists, we are essentially religious. And that is because God is the ground of all being. God is the meaningfulness in the midst of swirling chaos. God is the heart of every human being.

The Gospel of John knows this. John begins his Gospel by saying, "In the beginning was the Word, and the Word was with God, and the Word was God." In other words, in the beginning God expressed God's self, and everything comes into being through God's self-expression. *Everything* comes into being through the Word. Without the Word not one thing came into being.

So the Word of God is at the essence of every piece of reality—every stone, every blade of grass, every atom, every quark, every quantum.

Carl Jung, the great psychoanalyst, was once asked, "Do you believe there is a God?" Jung sputtered at the question and answered, "No, I don't believe there is a God, I *know* there is a God." In his book, *Modern Man in Search of a Soul*, he writes:

> Among all my patients in the second half of life, that is, over thirty-five, there has not been one whose problem in the last resort was not that of finding a religious outlook on life. It is

safe to say that every one of them fell ill because he had lost that which the living religions of every age have given their followers, and none of them has really been healed who did not regain his religious outlook.[1]

The bird is singing. Can you hear it? Will you feed it?

But how do we hear the song? How do we feed the bird? How do we recover our religious center when we're surrounded by a society that's deaf and has no religious center? Paul, in one of his letters, gives the early Christians the answer: "Pray without ceasing."

Wait a minute. What do you mean, "pray without ceasing"? How can anyone pray without ceasing, without ever stopping? If Paul meant, "verbally pray all the time," you're right, that's impossible. But I don't think that's what he meant. I think he meant be constantly aware of God. Let God be present to you at all times, and put yourself in the presence of God all the time.

Islam is a very interesting religion. To be a good Muslim you have to do only four things: (1) you have to believe there is only one God and Muhammad is his prophet, (2) you have to fast for one month every year, (3) you have to—if you can afford it—make a pilgrimage to Mecca sometime in your life, and (4) you have to pray five times a day.

This prayer rug comes from Saudi Arabia. It has a compass in it so the rug can be pointed toward Mecca. Five times a day every member of Islam, no matter where he is, no matter what she is doing, unrolls their prayer rug, orients it toward Mecca, kneels down, and says certain prayers.

This is a marvelous way to keep your religious center, because five times a day—no matter what you're doing—you are reminded of God and you put yourself in the presence of God. Members of Islam frequently criticize Western Christians because our religion is so private, so separated from jobs and recreation, and is expressed only one day a week—if even then. The members of Islam are right. Western Christians as a whole are pathetic. Our spiritual consciousness is terrible. We have been utterly seduced by a secular society that compels us to make our religion private, invisible, and put in a little compartment.

We can all learn something from Islam. For one thing, I suggest we all begin praying five times a day. Before you all go, "Oh, no, that's impossible, that's fanatical!"—no it's not. Listen: when you wake up, say, "Thank you, God, for the gift of another day. I give you my life. Do your will through me today." At breakfast, before you eat, say, "Thank you, God, for this food you provide." At lunch say, "Thank you, God, for this food you provide." At supper say, "Thank you, God, for this food you provide." And before you go to bed, review the day, tell God what you wish you had done differently, ask for forgiveness and new strength, and then say, "And now, God, use my sleep and dreams to restore me to your service."

That's it—five prayers a day. It's simple. The point is not to have long prayers. I don't believe in long prayers—especially if they're verbal prayers. But I do believe in shooting regular arrows to God, brief words from the heart, which keep us in the presence of God. So I don't care if you're at McDonald's or the employee's lounge—shoot those arrows to God. Do *not* allow a secular culture to shove your prayers to one day a week or only at your own dinner table. For *God's* sake, acknowledge God regularly every day.

The other main way we can recover our religious center and feed the bird is by coming together as believers *at least* every week. This is how we reinforce the song. This is how we reinforce the commitment to feed the bird in the midst of a society that doesn't care. If you do not come together every week to nurture Christ at your center, you will almost certainly lose that center, because otherwise you are surrounded by a soulless society that is pulling you in the opposite direction.

Many people have said to me, "I can worship God in the woods; I don't need church." Right, you can worship God in the woods, and in your house, and at the restaurant. That's not the point. Without a *religious* community to keep you religiously centered, the secular community will almost inevitably make you secularly centered.

This summer many of you have been cooking on the grill over hot coals. You know that if you separate the hot coals, they get cold faster. The same happens to us. We need each other to stay hot. That's a sociological, psychological, and spiritual fact.

Because of this, weekly church participation will always be top priority for my family—not because I'm the pastor, but because I'm a Christian who needs to stay hot and who has a responsibility to help others stay hot. Are there jobs that sometimes make weekly participation impossible? Yes. Are there important events that sometimes fall on Sunday morning? Yes. But I've made a personal decision that my son and my daughter will not be involved in any activity that interferes with church more than three or four times in a year. Do we want to be religiously centered, or centered on something else? That's the question.

In the second century an anonymous Christian wrote a letter addressed to the Roman emperor to defend the Christian faith. In that letter, this anonymous Christian described Christians in this way:

> For Christians cannot be distinguished from the rest of the human race by country or language or customs. They do not live in cities of their own; they do not use a peculiar form of speech; they do not follow an eccentric manner of life. . . . Yet, although they live in Greek and barbarian cities alike, as each man's lot has been cast, and follow the customs of the country in clothing and food and other matters of daily living, at the same time they give proof of the remarkable and admittedly extraordinary constitution of their own commonwealth. They

live in their own countries, but only as aliens. They have a
share in everything as citizens, and endure everything as for-
eigners. Every foreign land is their fatherland, and yet for them
every fatherland is a foreign land. They marry, like everyone
else, and they beget children, but they do not cast out their off-
spring. They share their board with each other, but not their
marriage bed. It is true they are "in the flesh," but they do not
live "according to the flesh." They busy themselves on earth,
but their citizenship is in heaven. They obey the established
laws, but in their own lives they go far beyond what the laws
require. They love all men, and by all men are persecuted.
They are unknown, and still they are condemned; they are put
to death, and yet they are brought to life. They are poor, and
yet they make many rich; they are completely destitute, and yet
they enjoy complete abundance. . . .

To put it simply: What the soul is in the body, that
Christians are in the world. The soul is dispersed through all
the members of the body, and Christians are scattered through
all the cities of the world. The soul dwells in the body, but
does not belong to the body, and Christians dwell in the world,
but do not belong to the world.[2]

We are the soul of the world. We are different from the
world. We have a different center than the world has. But
because we have that center, we help animate the world.

There's an old West African story about a man who married a maiden who had come down from the sky. The sky
maiden had consented to marry the man on the condition
that he never look inside a box that she had brought with
her. The man agreed, and for many years they were married.
But then one day when his wife was gone, the man's curiosity got the better of him and he opened up the box. Just then
his wife returned and found him with the opened box.
Sheepishly he confessed that he had opened the box, but that
he had found nothing inside. The sky maiden cried and
began packing her bags to leave. The man pleaded with her
to stay, again apologizing for opening the box. But she said
to him, "I'm not leaving because you opened the box. I knew

that someday you would. I'm leaving because you said it was empty. It is not empty—it is full of sky. How can I be your wife if what is most precious to me is emptiness to you?"

All of us who belong to Christ, who have been born, not by blood or by the will of the flesh, but by God, carry a box. In it is heaven. Others say it's nothing, but we know it's heaven. We bind ourselves together with others who carry that box. And together we animate the world.

My next sermon uses an entirely different format: dramatic dialogue. The book of Jonah concludes with a dialogue between God and Jonah. I decided to expand that dialogue into a full-length sermon, exploring the moral and theological implications of the story. By making God a dialogue partner, and addressing current concerns, the preacher creates the impression of God talking to us. This is prophetic preaching in its starkest form, and yet it uses a format (dramatic dialogue) that is familiar and acceptable to our culture. At the conclusion of the dramatic dialogue (in which I played Jonah), I once again became the preacher and pulled together the themes of the sermon to address a specific and current issue.

I preached this sermon on August 13, 2000, at First Mennonite Church (Indianapolis). Earlier in the service I recited Luke 17:3-4.

Jonah and God: A Dialogue

Narrator (N) and God (G) are played by same, disembodied voice, offstage.

N: *(read Jonah 1:1-3)*

J: O Lord, you are my God. Even when I ran from you and got on a ship heading for Tarshish, you did not run from me. When a terrible storm came and almost sunk our ship, you were still with me. When I told the sailors to throw me overboard, sacrificing my life, you did not desert me. Even as I was drowning, sinking in the depths of the sea, you rescued me with a mighty fish. For three days and three nights you protected me in the belly of that fish. And then you gave me a second chance to fulfill my calling. For this I am so grateful, Lord. And I *did* fulfill my calling. I proclaimed to the people of Nineveh the words you gave me. I shouted at the top of my lungs: "Forty days from now the true God, the God of Israel, will destroy your city!" You heard me proclaim your message. I said everything just as you wanted. . . . But Lord, forty days have now come and gone, and still Nineveh stands. Why have you not fulfilled your word?

G: *(long pause)* I changed my mind.

J: I'm sorry, Lord, I'm not sure I caught that. What did you say?

G: I changed my mind.

J: You . . . changed your mind?

G: That's right.

J: But Lord, you're God. You don't change. It's not proper. You can't change your mind!

G: Well, I did.

J: But what about your word? What about your message promising to destroy Nineveh in forty days? Don't you have to keep your word?

G: I changed my mind.

J: Lord, wait a minute. Don't be hasty. This is a test, right? You're just testing my faith or something, right?

G: No, I'm not testing your faith, Jonah. *I changed my mind.*

J: But, but, Lord . . . why?

G: Because the Ninevites changed *their* minds. Didn't you see all the people of Nineveh responding to your message? Didn't you see them praying to me and saying how sorry they were for being so violent? And didn't you see them humbling themselves by fasting and wearing sackcloth? Why, even the cows are all wearing sackcloth! They've changed their minds, so I've changed my mind. I'm not going to destroy them after all.

J: Lord, you're joking!

G: I'm not joking.

J: You're really not going to destroy them?

G: No, I'm not.

J: You're going to let those murderers go?

G: I'm not going to destroy them.

J: Lord, I don't mean to be disrespectful. I mean, please don't take this the wrong way, but you're so naive! Do you *really* think those people in Nineveh have *really* changed their minds? Do you think all their crying and praying and fasting and sackcloth is genuine repentance? It's a foxhole conversion! They're only doing it because they're scared of being blasted! Their sorriness is as thin as tissue! Five days from now they're going to be back to murdering again!

G: Do you know that or are you just guessing?

J: Well, I don't *know* that. I'm not God . . .

G: Exactly.

J: But God, come on, it can't be genuine. Their change of heart is too quick. Too convenient. It's got to be a scam!

G: I have looked in their hearts. I see genuine humility, genuine regret, and a genuine desire to change their behavior.

J: Yes, but for how long?

G: *(no answer)*

J: God, all right, all right—I'm not God. You can see into their hearts, I cannot. So let's just say their change of heart is genuine. It still doesn't matter, because this is a perversion of justice. Just because they're sorry, just because they fast and put on sackcloth, doesn't mean they should be let off the hook. They invade the lands of their neighbors, burning down villages, stealing food from the fields, and murdering helpless men, women, and children. They show no mercy. These are terrorists! These are mass murderers!

G: They aren't now.

J: That doesn't matter! They have been! And you're going to let them get away with it?

G: I'm not going to destroy their city.

J: *(pausing out of frustration)* God, let's be reasonable. Let's say a man is caught who murdered his wife and three children. He chopped them up and stuffed them in a freezer. And he did it just because he was tired of them. But let's say, while he's on trial, he starts feeling really bad about what he's done. He cries a lot. He says he was abused as a boy and didn't know any better. And he tells the judge he's really, really sorry. Then the judge says, "Well, since you're sorry, I'll let you go. Case dismissed!" Is that justice, God? Because that's what you're doing. You're freeing a murderer because he says he's sorry. No jail time. No punishment.

G: There are other kinds of punishment than destroying them.

J: What do you mean?

G: I'm not going to destroy their city and take away their lives. But they still have to live with their regret for all the pain they've caused. They still have to face their responsibilities and make amends to their neighbors. They can't do that if I kill them all.

J: Feeling regret isn't much of a punishment, God. Nor is making amends. Besides, how are they to make amends anyway? How are they to bring back the lives of the children they murdered? You got an answer for that, God?

G: *(pause)* So Jonah, you're saying that since they killed people, I must kill them. No chance for repentance, no chance for change, no chance for making amends, no chance for becoming a blessing in this world instead of a curse.

J: *(pause)* I think I'm beginning to see where you're coming from. All right, maybe I was a bit hasty. Maybe I was allowing my own hatred for the Ninevites to cloud my judgment. I hear you saying that now that the people of Nineveh have repented, now that they've committed themselves to being a peaceful people, they can do a lot of good in the world. But if you destroy them, all the good they *could* do would never happen. Is that it?

G: I think you're catching on.

J: So, Lord, what you're saying is that the Ninevites have a glorious future—they're going to become a great blessing to the earth.

G: *(no response)*

J: That is what you're saying, right? The Ninevites are going to become wonderful people who will do tremendous good in the world. If that's the case, I can understand you changing your mind. I think I can accept that.

G: That's not what's going to happen, Jonah.

J: Well what is going to happen? What's the future for the people of Nineveh?

G: Are you sure you want to know?

J: Yes!

G: *(pause)* The fact is, Jonah, forty years from now the people of Nineveh will invade your own country, Israel, and totally destroy it. Many of the Israelites will die, and many others will be deported to live in the empire of the Ninevites. Israel will be no more.

J: God, this can't be!

G: It will be.

J: So the Ninevites won't become a blessing to the world?

G: No.

J: I thought you said their change of heart was genuine.

G: It is . . . for now. But in another generation they will turn to evil once again.

J: Then why save them now? Destroy them! Kill them before they kill Israel!

G: Would you have me destroy repentant people?

J: But their repentance won't last!

G: That doesn't matter. They're repentant now.

J: But God, other innocent people will die if you don't destroy Nineveh soon. Sometimes you need to kill some in order to save others!

G: That's not my nature, Jonah. I am merciful and gracious.

J: I know, I know. You're "merciful and gracious, slow to anger and abounding in steadfast love"—I've heard it all before. I *have* read the Old Testament, you know. In fact, God, *this is why I ran away from you to begin with*. I *knew* you might let those Ninevites off the hook! I knew you'd find some excuse to be merciful and give them your undeserved grace. Well it isn't fair! Grace isn't fair! It's a rotten theological idea, so get rid of it!

G: Jonah, if I were fair—if I didn't show mercy to those who don't deserve it—we wouldn't be having this conversation now.

J: What do you mean?

G: Did you deserve to be saved by the fish? Didn't you disobey me and run away? And didn't you try to kill yourself by having the sailors throw you overboard? But I saved you. You didn't deserve it.

J: That was different.

G: How was it different?

J: My sins aren't as bad as the Ninevites. They're murderers, and they're going to murder again! That shouldn't receive mercy.

G: So you're better than they are?

J: You bet I am.

G: So you deserve my mercy and grace more than they do?

J: You bet I do.

G: *(pause)* It isn't grace or mercy if you deserve it, Jonah. *No one* deserves it. That's the whole point. That's what makes it so wonderful. That's what makes it so needed. Everyone needs my free gift of grace, or you're all goners.

J: *(pause)* Just leave me alone, God. Just leave me alone. I want to die. Don't save me this time. I don't want grace. I'm done with grace. *(walks out)*

N: *(read Jonah 4:5-8)*

J: *(walking back in slowly)* Let me die, God. I've had enough. You win. You always win. Now let me die.

G: Why are you so depressed about the death of a mere plant?

J: It gave me some shade. It was a bit of life out in this desert, a bit of green, a bit of hope.

G: And you feel pity for it, now that it's dead and gone.

J: Yes, I pity the plant's death.

G: Jonah, you pity a mere plant, a tiny bit of life that you didn't plant or cause to grow. Well I pity the people of Nineveh. There's a lot more life in that city than in that plant. And I created all those people. I have fed them and looked over them, and I have given them their every breath. Whether they do evil or good, I am their parent, and I love them.

J: God, I'm not really—

G: *(interrupting)* No, Jonah, listen! I pity those people in Nineveh. Frankly, they're a big disappointment to me, and it hurts me deeply—more deeply than you will ever know. They're like little children who never quite grew up. They do wrong, but they don't see it. They're stunted and immature because an evil worm has gotten inside of them, preventing their growth. So I pity them. I will not destroy them because they are still human beings with my life in them. Is there no pity in you for these sick people?

J: God, you're asking too much.

G: Am I, Jonah?

A historical note: About one hundred fifty years later the city of Nineveh was destroyed by the Babylonians. Evil behavior, if continued, always destroys itself. One evil always eventually destroys another evil. Evil behavior is inherently unstable; it is not sustainable; it will crumble from its own weight.

Because we tell the story of Jonah so often to children, we may forget that it's actually a story for adults. It's a tough story. I think at the heart of the story is this question: Is repentance sufficient for forgiveness? How do we know if repentance is genuine? How do we know if repentance is deep enough that it will result in fundamentally changed behavior? How do we know if repentance will last? The story of Jonah tells us we don't know.

But mercy is not based on a calculation of repentance. In the final analysis, God is merciful because God pities us—victims and offenders alike. Can we do the same? Will we do the same? Or will we demand the ultimate vengeance and take away any chance for repentance, any chance for change, any chance for good coming out of the offender? Will we execute the murderers?

This past summer a particular denomination went on record supporting the death penalty. Perhaps they have not considered the story of Jonah—or other Scriptures for that matter. As Paul says, quoting from the Old Testament, "'Vengeance is mine, I will repay, says the Lord.' No, 'if your enemies are hungry, feed them; if they are thirsty, give them something to drink; for by doing this you will heap burning coals [of remorse] on their heads.' "

One time I preached a series of sermons at First Mennonite Church (Indianapolis) on various Old Testament prophets. These sermons were expository, explaining each prophet's historical context and original meaning, as well as prophetic. As the series progressed, I experienced myself becoming increasingly bold, speaking more specifically and critically about current issues than I usually do. I have never felt more like a prophet than when I was preaching those sermons. I preached two sermons on Amos. The first one focused on Amos himself, and the next one, reproduced here, focused on the main theme of his message. I preached it on June 13, 1999.

Is Amos Speaking to Us?

Key Text: Amos 5:21-24

A friend of mine named Chuck is in the chicken business. His family owns several KFC franchises as well as operates its own chicken restaurant. One day Chuck told me about a friend of his who decided to also get into the chicken restaurant business. He lined up a chicken supplier who gave him a good price on chicken, set up his restaurant, and started his business. But as the months went by, he kept losing money. He was getting plenty of business, lots of customers, but he was still, somehow, losing money. So he went to Chuck and asked him, "What am I doing wrong?" Chuck looked over his balance sheets and asked, "Do you weigh the chicken shipments you receive?" The friend said, "No, the supplier weighs it." Chuck told him, "No, no, no—*always* weigh your chicken when it comes in." So, the next shipment that came in, he weighed it. And instead of it weighing, say, fifteen tons, it was twelve tons. The man got on the phone to his supplier and said, "Hey, I just weighed that last shipment of chicken and it wasn't full weight." The supplier answered, "Aw now, if you're going to weigh those chickens, I'm going to have to charge you more."

"Let justice roll down like waters, and righteousness like an everflowing stream."

The prophet Amos had a simple message: The Northern Kingdom of Israel will be destroyed. Its people will be butchered, or carried off into slavery, and its king will die a violent death. And God will allow all of this to happen.

And why will God allow such a horrendous fate to come upon Israel? Listen to Amos's indictment: "Thus says the Lord: For three transgressions of Israel, and for four, I will not revoke the punishment; because they sell the righteous for silver, and the needy for a pair of sandals—they who trample the head of the poor into the dust of the earth, and push the afflicted out of the way . . . they lay themselves down beside every altar on garments taken in pledge; and in the house of their God they drink wine bought with fines they imposed."

In other words, the reason why Israel is going to be destroyed is because the rich are taking advantage of, and oppressing, the poor. For instance, anyone who can't pay his debts, even if it's only as much as the price of a pair of sandals, gets sold into slavery. Instead of forgiving debts, or giving the poor a break, the rich who have loaned money to them are taking advantage of their inability to pay by making them into slaves.

Another thing that is going on is that the poor have to hand over their cloaks as a guarantee that they'll repay their debts, and they aren't getting their cloaks back at the end of the day. Moses' law forbids keeping a poor man's cloak after nightfall because the cloak is one's blanket, and sometimes it's the only thing that keeps a poor person from freezing in the night.

And in general the rich are imposing heavy fines on the common people.

From other passages in Amos we learn that the merchants are using false weights in the marketplace when they sell goods to the common people. And when they sell wheat, they're mixing in dust and scraps swept up from the floor.

To put it simply: People are not being treated fairly and equally. The rich are not doing justice. And the result will be that God will destroy their nation.

As I reread the book of Amos this week, I asked myself, "What's Amos's message for us? How does it apply to us? *Does* it apply to us?" And at first I thought, "Maybe not." After all, we've done away with slavery. No one goes to prison, or into slavery, because they can't pay debts. And although the marketplace is filled with companies that aren't completely honest, we have lots of federal regulations and consumer watchdog groups that try to keep fraud at a minimum. And certainly no one here rips off his customers. So a part of me says, "Maybe this doesn't apply to us. We're not doing these things Amos is condemning."

Well, we may not be doing *exactly* the things Amos was condemning in his day, but in our own way we *are* a society in which the rich exploit the poor.

Following World War II, America's economy boomed, and all levels of society—upper class, middle class, and lower class—benefited from that economic boom. But in the last two decades, while our economy has continued to be quite strong, the rich have gotten a lot richer and the poor poorer. From 1979 to 1994 the richest 5 percent of Americans saw their net worth increase by 45 percent. During that same period, the bottom 20 percent of wage earners saw their income drop by 13 percent.[3] Even the middle class has not benefited. While median family income has remained about the same for the last twenty years, that's only because far more families now have both spouses working. So even though we're living in a time of impressive economic growth and wealth, it is the richer half of society, especially the very top, that's getting much richer while the middle class is getting squeezed and the lower class is actually poorer than before.

How can this be? This will always inevitably happen whenever government is not curbing the benefits of the rich. The rich and big business have the clout to lobby for laws that benefit them. And right now we're in a time when it's fashionable to blame the poor for being poor and cut resources that provide help for them. President Clinton recently attempted to get the minimum wage raised so that a full-time worker wouldn't be below the poverty level. Congress easily defeated it.

Amos was telling the political leaders of his day: "It is *your* responsibility to protect the rights and needs and interests of the poor. It is your responsibility to restrain the power of the powerful who otherwise always get their way."

And from a global perspective, the injustices today are even greater. Our nation is by far the most powerful on this planet, and because it is, it tends to call the shots—militarily, politically, and economically. There's a reason why we're so wealthy compared to the rest of the world. There's a reason why we have every type of food and product available to us at a cheap price while the rest of the world often gets less of it at a higher price. It's *not* because we work harder. It's not because we're economically smarter than other nations. The reasons are complex and many, but one of them is that we are more powerful, and we use that power to favor us.

Our clothes and cars and VCRs are oftentimes made by people whose standard of living we would consider deplorable. They're glad for the jobs because they have no choice. Big business has them over a barrel. We exploit the poor at will. Michael Jordan was making more money for one Nike commercial than all the Malaysian workers manufacturing Nikes were making together for a year.

Last year one hundred and twenty nations voted to create an International Criminal Court. Genocide, war crimes, and other crimes against humanity would be brought to an international court so that all nations would be held equally accountable. One hundred twenty nations voted for it. Seven voted against it: China, Iraq, Iran, Libya, Sudan, Israel, and the USA. Why did the United States vote against it? Because it was afraid American soldiers might be tried some day at an international court. We want to control and punish our own—or maybe not punish them at all. Jesse Helms said any international court that could conceivably prosecute Americans would be "dead on arrival" on Capitol Hill. The only way the United States government would support an International Criminal Court was if the United States had veto power to block prosecution of Americans.[4] That's justice?

We may not be committing the exact same sins of the Northern Kingdom of Israel in the eighth century B.C., but we are, in our own powerful, callous, blind way, exploiting the poor and perverting justice. It doesn't matter if individually we're nice people, or that we go to church and say we're religious. As Amos says, "I hate, I despise your festivals, and I take no delight in your solemn assemblies. Even though you offer me your burnt offerings and grain offerings, I will not accept them; and the offerings of well-being of your fatted animals I will not look upon. Take away from me the noise of your songs; I will not listen to the melody of your harps."

Because we live in a democracy with elected representatives, we—you and I—are responsible for the political and economic policies of our government. We are responsible for the injustices that are sometimes promoted by our society. We may not ignore these injustices, blaming them on others, and worship God with a clean heart. Instead, we must use our money and e-mail, our voice and votes, to let justice roll down like waters, and righteousness like an everflowing stream.

A rabbi and his disciples were working out in a field one morning, far from the village. At noon, food and water were brought from the village. The disciples took a gourd of water to the rabbi so he could wash his hands and ritually purify himself. The rabbi dropped two drops of water on each hand—certainly not enough to clean off the dirt, and it was questionable whether two drops on either hand qualified as a ritual cleansing proscribed by the law. His disciples said, "Rabbi, why did you use so little water?" He pointed to a servant girl who had carried the water from the village. She was bent over low with a bar across her shoulders and two big pails of water hanging on either side. The rabbi answered, "The water I save may save her one trip to the well."

We too, by our daily choices, can save her a trip to the well.

This last sermon is the most expository of all, focusing on and explaining one particular biblical text. But in addition to being expository, it is also profoundly prophetic because it speaks an authoritative word straight from the living Jesus Christ to my congregation. Many mainline Protestant denominations include in the worship service a confession read by the congregation followed by a pronouncement of forgiveness read by the pastor. Such a ritual is very rare among Mennonites. We sometimes have confessional readings, but almost never a pronouncement of forgiveness. The reason is simple: in standard Mennonite theology, forgiveness results from genuine repentance and amendment of behavior. Thus, blanket forgiveness cannot be pronounced on a group of people simply because they have read some words on a page; the pastor has no way of knowing whether any of the expressions of repentance are genuine or not. This does not mean that Mennonite pastors do not pronounce God's grace on a congregation. They often do. But Mennonites make an important distinction between grace and forgiveness. Grace is God's freely given unconditional love. It is God's most basic attitude toward us and is not dependent on or effected by our response. On the other hand, forgiveness is the overcoming of our sin and experiencing reconciliation with God. It is initiated by God's grace, but completed by our repentance.

With this in mind, the reader will better appreciate the unusual proclamation of the following sermon. I preached it on January 9, 2000, at First Mennonite Church in Indianapolis.

All Is Forgiven

Key Text: Mark 2:1-12

When I was attending seminary, I worked at a nearby church as an assistant pastor. One of the members of the church was a man who previously had been convicted of child molesting. He had spent about three years in prison. After he was released, he returned to the church. Some people told the pastor that he should tell the man he wasn't welcome anymore, but the pastor opened his arms to the man.

The man joined the church choir, and some people told the pastor they'd leave the church if the man continued singing in the choir. The pastor told them, "Go ahead and leave, but he stays in the choir." I remember one Sunday when the choir was singing, and this man sang a solo about grace. It was very touching.

I got to know this man, his wife, and their two small children. I liked them.

About a year after I left that church, I was visiting with the pastor. He asked me, "Did you hear what happened to George? His children found him in the garage. He had turned on the car engine and committed suicide. He left a note that said, 'I just couldn't face the shame any longer.'"

One of our greatest needs in life is to be forgiven. All of us have, buried in our memories or repressed in our subconscious, things we have done we wish we had never done, and things we've said we wish we'd never said. It doesn't have to be a terrible crime—like murder or molesting—just a vicious word, a put down, a lie, a little cheating, a theft, an act of unfaithfulness, a broken promise. We tell ourselves it doesn't matter. We pretend it's no big deal. But when we're by ourselves, the memories come back and we feel ashamed.

I think everybody carries within them a part of themselves they've never been able to accept, never been able to forgive. For most people the result is low self-esteem, at least in certain vulnerable areas. For some the result is depression. For a few, the result is actual physical illness—a guilt so strong it makes us ill. And in the most extreme cases, the result of not finding forgiveness is suicide.

To truly be well, to truly be free and healthy and able to live to the fullest, we need forgiveness.

A man was paralyzed. We don't know what parts of his body were paralyzed—maybe just his legs, but probably his arms too because people had to carry him around on a cot. His friends hear that the great teacher is in town. People say he's got the power of God in him and heals all kinds of illnesses. The friends tell the paralyzed man, "We think this guy can help. We're taking you to him!"

They carry him on his cot to a little house where people are jammed inside, listening to the great teacher. A crowd is even pressed around the door, trying to hear from outside. No way can they get this paralyzed man and his cot in there to the teacher. But nothing's going to stop these friends! I think they must have been teenagers because of their flexible thinking. They came up with one of those ideas that sounds like a college prank: they climbed up on the thatched roof, got some ropes, pulled up the paralyzed guy on his cot, dug a massive hole in the thatched roof, and lowered their friend, on his cot, through the roof, right in front of Jesus.

Jesus must have laughed! Imagine the delight in his eyes and the smile on his face when he sees these friends doing this outlandish thing, just so they can get their friend in front of him. And Jesus looks at this paralyzed man and, instead of physically healing him, he does something even more profound. He says, "Son, your sins are forgiven!"

Now there are some scribes there, and they're the Bible experts. And they're quite offended by this statement by Jesus. "What do you mean you forgive him? Only God can forgive sins." This paralyzed man hadn't sinned against Jesus. If he had, Jesus could forgive him for those sins. But no, Jesus is forgiving him for *all* sins committed against anybody, anywhere, anytime. You can't do that! Besides, the Bible makes it quite clear how sins are forgiven. You must have a contrite heart, be sorry for your sins, and demonstrate that sorriness by offering a sacrifice at the temple. This paralyzed man hasn't offered any sacrifice. He hasn't even confessed any sins, or expressed any regrets, or made any commitments to change. He's done *nothing* to warrant forgiveness.

But Jesus forgives him anyway. Jesus, by doing this, is claiming to act for God, in God's place as God's representative. And Jesus says, in effect, "My son, even though you've made no confession and expressed no repentance and made no sacrifice, in the name of God I forgive you of all sins!"

No wonder the scribes went bonkers. No wonder they called it blasphemy. Of course, the scribes don't believe the man is *really* forgiven. Just because Jesus *says* he's forgiven doesn't *make* him actually forgiven. And Jesus knows this is what they're thinking, so he has to show them, in some visible way, that this man really is forgiven. So Jesus says, "To show you that I do indeed have God's authority to forgive sins, watch this: Stand up, take your cot, and go home." And the paralyzed man immediately, no problem, stood up, picked up his cot, and walked out.

In the Babylonian Talmud it says, "No sick person is cured of his disease until all his sins are forgiven him." In the ancient world it was assumed that illness is due, at least in part, to sin. And so if someone is healed, it must mean his or her sin is also forgiven. Remember that one time Jesus' disciples asked him about a blind man: "Is this man blind because he sinned or his parents sinned?" And in the Old

Testament, Job is perplexed by his illness because he can't figure out what his sin is. Now, Jesus did not assume that all illness was due to sin, but he did share this view with others: physical healing is a sign that spiritual healing has already taken place. So when Jesus healed a person, more than just a physical healing is taking place: it's a visible way of saying, "You are forgiven." Healing shows you are forgiven—no sin stands between you and God.

Frankly, this is why Jesus heals so many people in his ministry. It's not because he's a frustrated doctor; it's not even because he can't stand to see human disease. His purpose is deeper and greater. He wants to show people: God is forgiving you! All barriers between you and God are gone! You are free! Your *soul* is healed!

How can we be forgiven? In the Bible, the normal way to find forgiveness—whether with God or with others—is to confess what we've done wrong, express genuine regret, and, when appropriate, make restitution. That's essentially it. It's not very complicated, but it does take courage. It takes courage and honesty to confess your sins, express regret, and take responsibility. This is the normal process, and it is a wonderful process. It calls for honesty and responsibility from us—the offender, and it calls for unconditional caring and some mercy from the victim.

But sometimes we need more than this normal process. What if we are sinning and we don't know we are sinning? What if, out of our convictions and conscience, we do things that are actually wrong and destructive? What if we are harming the poor or the environment without realizing it? What if we are so blind we cannot see our own selfishness? What if we can't see how our words and actions are hurting others? Or what if we're caught in addictions where we keep repeating the same sins over and over? Or what if our heart is so wounded and so hardened we've never been able to properly confess and feel regret?

Sometimes, in rare instances, God needs to go beyond the normal process and be ridiculously generous and forgive us for everything, even when we haven't confessed and haven't expressed regret. This paralyzed man confessed no sins and expressed no regret for sin, but Jesus forgives *all* his sins. Why? Because his *friends* had faith. His friends enthusiastically believed Jesus could help. And so Jesus forgives him, and proves it by giving him the power to walk.

Jesus, in his ministry, heals scores of people without confession, without regrets expressed, but his healings show they are forgiven. He forgave them simply because they came to him. They believed he could help. And Jesus, when crucified, says from the cross, "Father, forgive them, they don't know what they're doing." His enemies and executioners are laughing at him—no confession, no regret—but Jesus forgives them all.

This is not how forgiveness usually happens. Usually it involves our responsible acts of confession, regret, and commitment. But every once in a while all of us need to be forgiven of all those things in our soul we can't quite see, we can't quite get a hold of, we can't cast out. Sometimes God needs to just forgive us in our paralyzed helplessness.

I want to tell you something about my soul. When I'm by myself, early in the morning, late at night, memories pop into my head that cause me pain and embarrassment. The funny thing is, none of the memories are terrible things; they're just the simple mistakes and stupidities of life, all the little things I've done that were foolish or embarrassing. And I find myself kicking myself after each memory, putting myself down, condemning myself. In Chicago, where I grew up, there's an expressway called the Dan Ryan Expressway. Well, when I get on this string of memories in which I'm putting myself down over and over, I call it the Damn Ryan Expressway. And I want to get off that expressway. I want to get off.

I have a fantasy sometimes. I wonder what it would be like if all of us knew all of our secrets. What if everything we've ever done, ever thought, was known, and we knew everyone else's. What would happen? I think we would all sigh a tremendous sigh of relief, because we'd no longer need to hide anything because there'd be nothing left to hide. And we'd have discovered we're all much more alike than we'd ever imagined. And I think we'd all hug each other and say, "You're forgiven." It is said, "To know all is to forgive all." Certainly God knows all.

I believe God wishes to free all of us now, this morning. I believe Jesus' ministry of healing and forgiveness is not over, but is meant to continue in every church. I believe everyone here was brought by enthusiastic friends, family, or ancestors who believed Jesus could help. And so this morning, in the name of Jesus, I want you to hear what that paralytic heard, so you can walk and run and be free.

In the name of Jesus, all of you here are forgiven. Right now, everything you've ever done or said or thought or felt—it's all forgiven. God forgives you. For every put down and nasty thing you've said to your spouse or children or family or friends or enemies, God forgives you. For all the physical abuse, God forgives you. For all your prejudices and insensitivities and self-righteousness, God forgives you. For all your gossip and hate and resentments and evil thoughts, God forgives you. For all your foolishness and embarrassments and stupidity and mistakes, God forgives you. For all your stealing and addictions and abortions and exploitations and unfaithfulness, God forgives you. For everything big or little, in the name of Jesus, rise up, take your pallet and go home, because God forgives you.

We speak on Christ's behalf. We don't talk about what Christ said long ago. We don't talk about Christ. We speak for Christ. Christ speaks through us.

—Richard A. Jensen[1]

CHAPTER 9

Conclusions

In this succinct statement, Richard Jensen sums up my understanding of prophetic preaching. Ultimately our task as preachers is not to repeat the old word but to proclaim a new word for our people and our situation that is congruent with Scripture and faithful to Jesus Christ. The radical conclusion to this trajectory is that we are actually giving voice to God's ever-speaking Word. We become prophets, speaking directly God's Word for the congregation.

Why do we speak "with authority"? Is it for our own ego-needs? Is it so our congregations will rank us as great preachers? Absolutely not. In fact, such motivation undercuts the very possibility of speaking for God. The reason we dare to speak a new word with authority is because we see a world dominated by a reign of self-centeredness and fear while we ourselves have experienced the nearness and certainty of the reign of God. The world does not need a Christian history lesson; the world needs signs of God's subversive, hope-filled kingdom dawning among us.

So the goal of prophetic preaching is to enable people to move from self-centeredness to God-centeredness, from fear to courageous trust, from a slowly destructive lifestyle to a generous and healing way of life. In short, the goal of prophetic preaching is conversion. The evangelical tradition has always embraced this goal, and as a result it has developed a style of preaching which is direct, simple, and emotionally persuasive for many people. In addition, evangelical preaching is often accompanied by an altar call that gives opportunity for hearers to make a decision and public commitment. The mainline Protestant tradition might do well to examine this style more seriously.

But traditional evangelistic preaching also has its limitations. Sometimes it is simplistic about the meaning of salvation, boiling it down to a mental affirmation of certain doctrines and a verbal repetition of "the sinner's prayer." Sometimes it is emotionally manipulative, playing on infantile fears or joys to get decisions for Christ. Sometimes it embraces a gospel of fame and material success, using pop culture stars to market the faith. Sometimes it ignores the evil residing in our economic structures, believing that God's kingdom is a matter of personal morality alone. And the altar call itself reinforces a questionable understanding of conversion that is quick, focused on a particular time and place. As a result of these factors, I believe evangelistic conversions are often shallow, having little lasting impact on actual social behavior. Rates of abuse, divorce, and unethical business practices appear to be as high for the "born again" as for the general population. "Conversion" too often amounts to a continuation of society's status quo combined with innocuous religious practices and lip-service for Jesus.

In the face of such dismal results, some mainline Protestant homileticians have suggested it is unrealistic to make transformation the goal of the sermon.[2] Transformation (or conversion) is rare and almost always slow. Besides, it is arrogant and foolish for us to think we can transform anyone. Only God can. Thus, weekly preaching ought to have a more modest goal.

This is certainly a sensible word. If we are trying to fully convert people in every sermon, our sermons will become coercive, anxious, and shrill; any resulting conversions will likely be short-lived. Real, fundamental transformation of a person's perspectives, behaviors, values, and spiritual focus is a long process influenced by countless experiences. *But the sermon must be one of those experiences.* Our goal in prophetic preaching is not to transform everyone immediately (which will never happen anyway), but to transform some of them eventually. Our prophetic preaching is to have a cumulative effect, slowly enabling a new spiritual consciousness and faith accompanied by basic life changes.

But even a steady diet of patient prophetic preaching will become wearisome to a congregation if the focus of that preaching consists entirely of change. Weekly preaching to a largely static congregation is significantly different from Jesus' itinerant preaching to a constantly fluctuating crowd. The weekly needs of a congregation differ from the one-time needs of an anonymous audience. A congregation needs pastoral comfort as well as challenge. Prophetic preaching is often, but certainly not always, confrontive. God's prophetic word for us now also includes words of rest, consolation, and congratulation. "Blessed are you who weep now, for you will laugh" (Luke 6:21b). Preachers need to assess the right mix for their own congregations. For those times when preachers most need to challenge their congregations, one strategy worth considering is to invite guest speakers to preach prophetically, no holds barred. An outsider may be more free to offend and challenge the sacred (and idolatrous) cows of a congregation than is the pastor who must remain and work cooperatively within the congregation.

Do we change people? No. We plant and water, but leave the growth to God. Counting "conversions" and placing notches on one's Bible is delusional. If someone, following a sermon, requests baptism, that is the work of God and the result of many seeds sown over many years by many people.

On the other hand, the slowness of genuine transformation does not mean that we remove from our preaching the altar call—the opportunity for hearers to express their desires and commitments within the context of corporate worship. Without a public forum for expressing one's commitment, the believer lacks the public endorsement and ongoing encouragement and nurture of the community of faith. At some point conversion, if it is to be sustained, must be verbally or symbolically affirmed before the community. Provision must be made for hearers to make public their desire to die to themselves and live for God alone. Otherwise, conversion becomes a privatized experience, and without the support of the faith community it will likely be swallowed up by the dominant norms of society.

John the Baptist tapped into this need by offering baptism as a symbolic way for his hearers to respond to his preaching and demonstrate the fundamental change in their orientation. Jesus tapped into this need by challenging his listeners to symbolize their radical trust in God by selling all they possessed and joining Jesus in his itinerant ministry. Prophetic preaching today should likewise make available to hearers a physical way to express their faith and be supported by the community of faith. For those churches in the "believers church" tradition, baptism is the most powerful symbol that a person has truly been converted from self-centeredness to Christ-centeredness and that a transformed life is beginning. In such churches, prophetic preaching should facilitate hearers being able to respond and request baptism (which begins a preparation time lasting perhaps months or even years, as it did in the early church). For those churches that baptize infants, other rituals must be used that allow youth and adults to publicly confess their faith and symbolically enact the process of a genuine transformation.

The first sermon ever recorded in the early church does not end with the preacher sitting down and the congregation singing a hymn and then being dismissed. Rather, following Peter's Spirit-filled proclamation, the hearers "were cut to the heart and said to Peter and to the other apostles, 'Brothers, what should we do?'" (Acts 2:37). Prophetic preaching ought to open up the possibility of the congregation asking precisely this question, and the prophet had better have something concrete and challenging for them to do or an opportunity for ongoing conversion has been missed.

Dare to be as radical as Jesus. Overturn society's idolization of fame, wealth, status, and coercive power. Show them how to live out God's kingdom here on earth as it is in heaven.

Jesus once said, "Every scribe who has been trained for the kingdom of heaven is like the master of a household who brings out of his treasure what is new and what is old" (Matt. 13:52). We preachers are indeed scribes. Inside of our treasure box is a wealth of Scripture and a rich history of interpretation and critical tools. But if we are to be trained for the kingdom of God, enabling others to experience the reality of God's presence and power, then we will also need to bring out of our treasure box something new—a new word, God's ever-speaking Word, spoken through a prophet.

Ultimately, prophetic preaching is not about forms or techniques. It is about who we are. One day a friend of mine who was a pastor called me up and asked if he could have lunch with me. During lunch he somberly told me he was leaving the ministry. I was surprised and saddened; he was an admired and effective pastor. I asked him why he was giving up pastoral ministry. He answered, "I no longer have the words to speak." To preach like Jesus we must nurture a spiritual life utterly dependent on God that allows us to continue hearing God. After a day of healing and teaching, early the next morning Jesus "went out to a deserted place, and there he prayed" (Mark 1:35). After his disciples completed a successful teaching and healing mission of their own, Jesus told them, "Come away to a deserted place all by yourselves and rest a while" (Mark 6:31). A prophetic ministry spends more time in study, reflection, prayer, and cultivating total trust in God than it does in action. We must daily and consciously place ourselves in God's hands and empty ourselves of all fear and selfishness. By this we may experience the reality of God's reign around us and become instruments of God's Word in this world.

No form or technique can cover up character. Our most important task then, from now until we preach our last word, is to mature in Christ. We always keep in mind the words of the Catholic saint, Anthony Mary Claret: "If God's word is spoken only naturally, it does very little; but if it is spoken by a priest who is filled with the fire of charity—the fire of love of God and neighbor—it will wound vices, kill sins, convert sinners, and work wonders."[3]

Notes

Preface

1. Anthony de Mello, *The Song of the Bird* (New York: Doubleday, 1984), 32-3. Copyright © 1982 by Anthony de Mello, S.J. Used by permission of Doubleday, a division of Random House, Inc.

Chapter 1

1. Stanley Hauerwas, *A Community of Character: Toward a Constructive Christian Social Ethic* (Notre Dame, Ind.: University of Notre Dame Press, 1981).

2. The textbook which most helpfully explores the difference between teaching and proclaiming is by Richard Jensen, *Telling the Story: Variety and Imagination in Preaching* (Minneapolis: Augsburg Press, 1980).

Chapter 2

1. See Anthony J. Saldarini, "Scribes," in *The Anchor Bible Dictionary*, vol. 5, ed. D. N. Freedman (New York: Doubleday, 1992), 1012-6.

2. Throughout this book I will be referring to what Jesus did and said, fully realizing that historians disagree about what can be said about the historical Jesus. Most historians agree that the Jesus portrayed in the Gospels is not the same as the historical Jesus. For instance, the Jesus Seminar emphasizes the distance between the Jesus of the Gospels and the historical Jesus. See Robert Funk, R. Hoover, and the Jesus Seminar, *The Five Gospels: The Search for the Authentic Words of Jesus* (New York: Polebridge Press, 1993). I appreciate the Seminar's work and agree with many of their conclusions, but I think the distance between the synoptic (Matthew, Mark, Luke) Jesus and the historical Jesus has been exaggerated. Luke T. Johnson makes a compelling case that the most "real" Jesus is the one portrayed in the Gospels rather than the thin, hypothetical, and diverse reconstructions of historians. See Luke T. Johnson, *The Real Jesus: The Misguided Quest for the Historical Jesus and the Truth of the Traditional Gospels*

(San Francisco: HarperSanFrancisco, 1996). In my opinion, the best overall treatment of the historical Jesus is E. P. Sanders, *The Historical Figure of Jesus* (New York: The Penquin Press, 1993).

Some of the arguments I make in this book about Jesus do not need to have historical veracity. It is sufficient if my portrait agrees with how the earliest Christian communities understood the nature of Jesus' preaching. However, at times my argument does depend on the historical accuracy of my depiction of Jesus' preaching, and so I have sought to be informed of and judicious regarding the work of various historians. This assumed, my reconstruction of Jesus' preaching style is based on the Jesus portrayed in the first three Gospels. I will not make use of the Jesus portrayed in the Gospel of John since the teaching content, form, and mode differ so much from that found in Matthew, Mark, and Luke.

3. Bruce D. Chilton, *A Galilean Rabbi and His Bible: Jesus' Use of the Interpreted Scripture of His Time* (Wilmington, Del.: Michael Glazier, Inc., 1984), 141.

4. Ibid., 188.

5. Ibid., 187.

6. Robert M. Grant, *A Short History of the Interpretation of the Bible*, 2d ed. (Minneapolis: Fortress Press, 1984), 10.

7. To my knowledge, the best discussion of Jesus' understanding and treatment of the Mosaic Law is found in Harvey K. McArthur, *Understanding the Sermon on the Mount* (London: Epworth Press, 1960), 26-57. See also Sanders, *The Historical Figure of Jesus*.

8. Marcus Borg has proposed understanding the historical Jesus as, among other things, a sage who spoke proverbs of wisdom. See his *Jesus: A New Vision* (San Francisco: Harper & Row, 1987), and his more recent popular account, *Meeting Jesus Again for the First Time: The Historical Jesus and the Heart of Contemporary Faith* (San Francisco: HarperSanFrancisco, 1994).

Chapter 3

1. The Jesus Seminar overwhelmingly favors a noneschatological Jesus, and in my opinion this is one of the major flaws in their book, *The Five Gospels: The Search for the Authentic Words of Jesus* (New York: Polebridge Press, 1993). For two contrasting accounts of the historical Jesus, the first noneschatological and the second unabashedly eschatological and apocalyptic, see John Dominic Crossan, *Jesus: A Revolutionary Biography* (San Francisco: HarperSanFranciso, 1994) and Bart D. Ehrman, *Jesus: Apocalyptic Prophet of the New Millennium* (Oxford: Oxford University Press, 1999).

2. See John Dominic Crossan, *Cliffs of Fall: Paradox and Polyvalence in the Parables of Jesus* (New York: Seabury Press, 1980), 49.

3. One of the best overall discussions of the historical Jesus can be found in *Theology Today* 52:1 (April 1995).

4. See John Donahue, *The Gospel in Parable: Metaphor, Narrative, and Theology in the Synoptic Gospels* (Minneapolis: Augsburg Fortress Press, 1988), 214-5.

5. This is the argument of Bernard B. Scott, *Hear Then the Parable: A Commentary on the Parables of Jesus* (Minneapolis: Augsburg Fortress Press, 1989), 35. Scott's book is the best survey and analysis of all of Jesus' parables, and his introduction is especially enlightening.

6. This is the position of storyteller and theologian John Shea as related to me in conversation.

7. John Dominic Crossan, "Parable," in *The Anchor Bible Dictionary*, vol. 5, ed. D. N. Freedman (New York: Doubleday, 1992), 149.

8. John Dominic Crossan, *In Parables: The Challenge of the Historical Jesus* (New York: Harper & Row, 1973), 53. This little book, though somewhat dated, is the most exciting exploration of Jesus' parables I have read.

9. C. H. Dodd, *The Parables of the Kingdom* (New York: Charles Shribner's & Sons, 1961), 5.

10. Scott, *Hear Then the Parable*, xi.

11. Kenneth E. Bailey, *Through Peasant Eyes: More Lukan Parables, Their Culture and Style* (Grand Rapids, Mich.: Eerdmans, 1980), xi. Bailey's introduction is extremely helpful in differentiating between illustrations and parables.

12. Crossan, *In Parables*, 52.

13. Donahue, *The Gospel in Parable*, 13.

14. Elizabeth Achtemeir, *Creative Preaching* (Nashville: Abingdon Press, 1981), 24.

15. For instance, Luke interprets the Good Samaritan as a moral example of loving everyone, even a stranger or enemy. But if that was Jesus' intended meaning, then the Samaritan should have been the wounded man. Rather than being a moral example, the good Samaritan parable confronts us with the disturbing image of a hated outsider helping us—an image that overturns our prior judgments.

16. William Herzog, *Parables As Subversive Speech: Jesus As Pedagogue of the Oppressed* (Louisville, Ky.: Westminster/John Knox Press, 1994).

Chapter 5

1. Lamar Williamson Jr., *Mark*, Interpretation: A Bible Commentary for Teaching and Preaching, ed. James Luther Mays (Louisville, Ky.: Westminster/John Knox Press, 1983), 52.

2. For example, Lucy Atkinson Rose, *Sharing the Word*

(Louisville, Ky.: Westminster/John Knox Press, 1997). This book is a valuable survey and critique of the major American preaching styles of the 20th century. Rose seeks a style of preaching that is as dialogical and egalitarian as possible—what she calls "connected knowing."

3. According to *The Didache*, a church manual from the early second century, itinerant prophets were still active in the church (as was the need for congregations to discern their integrity). See *Early Christian Fathers*, ed. Cyril C. Richardson (New York: Macmillan Publishing, 1970), 176.

Chapter 6

1. See Paul Scott Wilson, *A Concise History of Preaching* (Nashville: Abingdon Press, 1992).

Chapter 7

1. See Robert Funk, *Language, Hermeneutic and the Word of God* (New York: Harper & Row, 1996), 196.

2. John Dominic Crossan, *In Parables: The Challenge of the Historical Jesus* (New York: Harper & Row, 1973), 36. Crossan groups Jesus' parables into similar categories: the advent of God's reign, its reversal of our world, and its empowerment for life and action, but he begins with a much larger pool of parables and he separates them differently than I do.

3. This chapter includes a few examples of parables of the kingdom of God that I have tried to create. For other (and better) examples of new parables in the spirit of Jesus, see Fred Craddock, *Overhearing the Gospel: Preaching and Teaching the Faith to Persons Who Have Already Heard* (Nashville: Abingdon Press, 1978), 36-7, 46, 89.

4. John Dominic Crossan, *The Dark Interval: Towards a Theology of Story* (Sonoma, Calif.: Polebridge Press, 1988), 87.

5. I am a Mennonite, and this story was originally created for a Mennonite congregation to hear. Menno Simons, who appears later, is the most revered of the early Mennonite leaders. The idea for this parable came from a joke I heard many years ago.

Chapter 8

1. Quoted by Harold Kushner, *When All You've Ever Wanted Isn't Enough: The Search for a Life That Matters* (New York: Summit Books, 1986), 177.

2. Cyril C. Richardson, ed., *Early Christian Fathers* (New York: Macmillan Publishing, 1970), 216-8.

3. These figures are based on an editorial, "Missing at the Table," *Christian Censtury* (7 April 1999): 379.

4. Douglass Cassel, "Why We Need the International Criminal Court," *Christian Century* (May 12, 1999): 532-5.

Chapter 9

1. Richard A. Jensen, *Thinking in Story: Preaching in a Post-Literate Age* (Lima, Ohio: C.S.S. Publishing, 1993), 73. In this excellent book, Jensen argues that because we live in a post-literate age, our preaching needs to "think in story" rather than thinking in ideas.

2. Lucy Atkinson Rose, *Sharing the Word* (Louisville, Ky.: Westminster/John Knox Press, 1997), 84.

3. Quoted by Jill Haak Adels, *The Wisdom of the Saints: An Anthology* (New York: Oxford University Press, 1987), 124.

Selected Bibliography

Ausubel, Nathan, ed. *A Treasury of Jewish Folklore*. New York: CrownPublishers, 1948.

Bailey, Kenneth E. *Through Peasant Eyes: More Lukan Parables, Their Culture and Style*. Grand Rapids, Mich.: Eerdmans, 1980.

Bailey, Raymond. *Jesus the Preacher*. Nashville: Broadman, 1990.

Bausch, William J. *Storytelling: Imagination and Faith*. Mystic, Conn.: Twenty-Third Publications, 1984.

Boomershine, Thomas E. *Story Journey: An Invitation to the Gospel as Storytelling*. Nashville: Abingdon, 1988.

Borg, Marcus. *Jesus: A New Vision*. San Francisco: Harper & Row, 1987.

_____. *Meeting Jesus Again for the First Time: The Historical Jesus and the Heart of Contemporary Faith*. San Francisco: HarperSanFrancisco, 1994.

Buechner, Frederick. *Telling the Truth: The Gospel as Tragedy, Comedy & Fairy Tale*. San Francisco: HarperCollins, 1977.

Chatfield, Donald F. *Dinner with Jesus and Other Left-Handed Story-Sermons: Meeting God Through the Imagination*. New York: Zondervan, 1988.

Chilton, Bruce D. *A Galilean Rabbi and His Bible: Jesus' Use of the Interpreted Scripture of His Time*. Wilmington, Del.: Michael Glazier, 1984.

Craddock, Fred. *Overhearing the Gospel: Preaching and Teaching the Faith to Persons Who Have Already Heard*. Nashville: Abingdon, 1978.

_____. *Preaching*. Nashville: Abingdon, 1985.

Crossan, John Dominic. *In Parables: The Challenge of the Historical Jesus*. New York: Harper & Row, 1973.

_____. *Cliffs of Fall: Paradox and Polyvalence in the Parables of Jesus*. New York: Seabury Press, 1980.

_____. *The Dark Interval: Towards A Theology of Story*. Sonoma, Calif.: Polebridge Press, 1988.

_____. *Jesus: A Revolutionary Biography*. San Francisco: HarperSanFrancisco, 1994.

De Mello, Anthony. *The Song of the Bird*. New York: Doubleday, 1984.

Donahue, John. *The Gospel in Parable: Metaphor, Narrative, and Theology in the Synoptic Gospels*. Minneapolis: Augsburg Fortress Press, 1989.

Ehrman, Bart D. *Jesus: Apocalyptic Prophet of the New Millennium*. Oxford: Oxford University Press, 1999.

Funk, Robert W., Roy W. Hoover, and the Jesus Seminar. *The Five Gospels: The Search for the Authentic Words of Jesus*. New York: Macmillan, 1993.

_____. *The Acts of Jesus: The Search for the Authentic Deeds of Jesus*. New York: HarperSanFrancisco, 1998.

Grant, Robert M. *A Short History of the Interpretation of the Bible*, 2d ed. Minneapolis: Fortress Press, 1984.

Hauerwas, Stanley. *A Community of Character: Toward a Constructive Christian Social Ethic*. Notre Dame, Ind.: University of Notre Dame Press, 1981.

Herzog, William. *Parables As Subversive Speech: Jesus as Pedagogue of the Oppressed*. Louisville, Ky.: Westminster/John Knox Press, 1994.

Jensen, Richard A. *Telling the Story: Variety and Imagination in Preaching*. Minneapolis: Augsburg Fortress Press, 1980.

_____. *Thinking in Story: Preaching in a Post-Literate Age*. Lima, Ohio: C.S.S. Publishing, 1993.

Johnson, Luke T. *The Real Jesus: The Misguided Quest for the Historical Jesus and the Truth of the Traditional Gospels*. San Francisco: HarperSanFrancisco, 1996.

Levin, Meyer, ed. *Classic Hassidic Tales*. New York: Penguin, 1975.

Lowry, Eugene L. *How to Preach a Parable: Designs for Narrative Sermons*. Nashville: Abingdon, 1989.

McArthur, Harvey K. *Understanding the Sermon on the Mount*. London: Epworth Press, 1960.

Meier, John P. *A Marginal Jew: Rethinking the Historical Jesus*, 2 vols. New York: Doubleday, 1991, 1994.

Rose, Lucy Atkinson. *Sharing the Word*. Louisville, Ky.: Westminster/John Knox Press, 1997.

Sanders, E. P. *The Historical Figure of Jesus*. New York: Penguin, 1993.

Scott, Bernard B. *Hear Then the Parable: A Commentary on the Parables of Jesus*. Minneapolis: Augsburg Fortress Press, 1989.

Shea, John. *Stories of God: An Unauthorized Biography*. Allen, Tex.: ThomasMore Press, 1978.

_____. *Stories of Faith*. Chicago: ThomasMore Press, 1980.

_____. *An Experience Named Spirit*. Allen, Tex.: ThomasMore Press, 1983.

_____. *The Legend of the Bells and Other Tales: Stories of the Human Spirit*. Chicago: ACTA Publications, 1996.

Steindl-Rast, Brother David. "The Grateful Heart." Audiotape. Albany, N.Y.: Abba House of Prayer, no date.

Troeger, Thomas H. *Imagining a Sermon*. Nashville: Abingdon, 1990.

Wallace, James A. *Imaginal Preaching: An Archetypal Perspective*. New York: Paulist Press, 1995.

White, William R. *Speaking in Stories: Resources for Christian Storytellers*. Minneapolis: Augsburg Fortress Press, 1982.

_____. *Stories for Telling: A Treasury for Christian Storytellers*. Minneapolis: Augsburg Fortress Press, 1986.

_____. *Stories for the Journey: A Sourcebook for Christian Storytellers*. Minneapolis: Augsburg Fortress Press, 1988.

Wilson, Paul Scott. *Imagination of the Heart: New Understandings in Preaching.* Nashville: Abingdon, 1988.

_____. *A Concise History of Preaching.* Nashville: Abingdon, 1992.

_____. *The Practice of Preaching.* Nashville: Abingdon, 1995.

The Author

PCA International

Ryan Ahlgrim is senior pastor at First Mennonite Church in Indianapolis, Indiana. He is a graduate of the Association of Chicago Theological Schools Doctor of Ministry in Preaching Program. He received his Doctor of Ministry from McCormick Theological Seminary. Ahlgrim and his wife, Laurie, are parents of two children, Garrett and Savannah.